LUCK BY DESIGN

THE SCIENCE AND SERENDIPITY OF A WELL-LIVED LIFE

ADAM TANK

TANK PRESS BOOKS

Book Cover by Austin Gray

To Kelsey & Briar—my reminders that life's greatest treasures are born from serendipity.

PART ONE
THE CATALYST EFFECT

CHAPTER 1
CHOOSE YOUR OWN ADVENTURE

When the eighteen-year-old received her ticket to Los Angeles, she was indignant.

"No," she protested. "I'm trying to get to *Hollywood*."

To the airline worker, the girl's confusion was endearing. As young as she'd seemed before he handed her the ticket, she seemed even younger now. With all the kindness he could muster, he explained that Hollywood was, in fact, in LA, and sent the lanky teenager off to chase her dream.

But the move to Los Angeles hadn't always been her dream. In fact, the idea had only recently flowered in her mind, blossoming from a seed she had never intended to sow.

Shortly before, she'd moved to Manhattan to become a dancer. The experience was harrowing. With very little money or support, she'd lived with a friend in a tiny apartment with no windows—a "shithole," she would later recall—while taking classes at the renowned Joffrey Ballet School.[1] She'd seen herself as a dancer for some time, despite the fact that her success had come not from ballet but from modeling.

A year or so before, the young woman had won a contest that sent her to Milan to model. From there, she toured Europe for a year. But she hadn't liked modeling; at least, not compared with the demands of the barre. She loved the practice it took to refine her movements on the ballet stage, tweaking a finger by a fraction of an inch and reaching just a little farther with the tip of a toe.

She'd always seen herself as a dancer—regardless of her career potential, it was her identity.

Then her knees went out.

It's difficult to overstate the psychological damage of losing one's identity. And for a young woman who had moved around the world to attend ballet school, the realization that she would never become a professional dancer was heart-wrenching.

Distraught, she sulked in her tiny apartment until her mother flew in from South Africa. "Either you figure out what to do next," she warned, "or you come home."[2]

But the teenager didn't want to come home. Stubborn and determined, she had dreams of stardom. She'd always loved movies, so she scraped together enough money for a one-way ticket to Los Angeles. A single suitcase held all of her belongings. Even that suitcase was worn, a tear appearing in its fabric during one leg of her international travel. She used a hairpin to mend the rip as best she could and boarded her flight to Hollywood.

It was 1994, the year the LA earthquake killed fifty-seven people, the year Kurt Cobain died, the year Shane Stant swung a baton into Nancy Kerrigan's knee. Around the time the teenager arrived in California, OJ Simpson would lead police on a low-speed chase along the 91 freeway.

When she got off the plane, she hopped into a cab and asked the driver to take her to the cheapest hotel in LA. In 1994 that was the Farmer's Daughter.

And in 1994 the Farmer's Daughter was the cheapest for a reason.

While the hotel had rooms for rent at an hourly rate, the girl took a room for $28 a day. She picked up a bottle of bleach and scoured the room, pausing from time to time to admire the Hollywood sign through her grungy window.

She used her modeling experience to sign with an agency, telling them that she didn't need to become a supermodel—she just needed jobs that paid. Because she was willing to take any job—including the catalogue modeling jobs most girls didn't want—she earned enough money to get by.

But barely.

As the little money she'd saved began to dry up, she realized her time was limited. She'd held on to her last New York modeling check, and as she tucked it into her purse and headed to the bank, she knew it was her last shot to make her own way—not her mother's—in the city.

FORCING ORDER ONTO CHANCE

It's Thursday afternoon, and you're wading through the week's emails when you hear a knock at your office door.

Leaning against the doorframe is your co-worker. "Did you hear?" she whispers conspiratorially. "I guess Deb has cancer. She's on leave starting next week."

Although you don't know Deb well, the news knocks you off balance. "Wow," is all you can manage to sputter.

"Lung cancer," your friend says somberly. "At least, that's what Manny said." Your co-worker stands there, leaning against the door frame for a few seconds, clearly thinking about the situation. Finally, she adds, "I didn't even think she smoked..."

The question—of whether or not a lung cancer patient smokes cigarettes—sounds harsh. Cancer is a horrific disease, and its victims deserve to be supported. And yet, in the context of a conversation about lung cancer, the question of smoking comes up almost inevitably.

It's not a matter of coincidence. It's a matter of psychology.

While cigarettes are strongly linked to lung cancer, many nonsmokers are diagnosed every year—up to 40,000 people, to be exact. At the same time, many smokers never develop the disease. Lung cancer, like all cancers, has a strong component of chance. We simply cannot know who will and who will not be diagnosed.

That's a big problem, particularly for our individual sense of personal security. It's difficult to reckon with the idea that a random chance occurrence could completely change our lives—and that we would be powerless to stop it.

This was Melvin J. Lerner's focus when he distilled two decades of psychological research in his landmark book, *The Belief in a Just World*.[3] Demonstrating his findings through a series of studies, he argued that our belief in a fair and just world serves a protective function. If we believe that the world is fundamentally *dis*ordered—that bad things happen randomly to all kinds of people, sometimes with permanent consequences—we feel constantly vulnerable. If, on the other hand, we can convince ourselves that bad things happen only to those who invite them, then we feel confident that we can avoid those negative outcomes, simply by taking stronger, more effective action than the victim in question.

Here's where the question of lung cancer comes in. When we believe we can control the ultimate outcome of a chance misfortune, we are more likely to accept that the misfortune was, in fact, by chance.

But in the case of something like lung cancer, the outcome is never guaranteed—it's not even controllable. That's why, in scenarios like Deb's, we often look for an explanation rooted in the victim's behavior.

The reason is simple: our ability to exert some level of control over a situation directly influences how we understand that situation, and for good reason—the illusion of control makes us feel safe. By assigning some responsibility to the victim, we assure ourselves that, if *we* were the victim, *we* would never allow the misfortune to occur in the first place.

If the victim could have prevented the injustice, then

we can prevent it, too. This makes the world feel like a much safer, much more predictable place. And there's nothing humans love like predictable safety.

This thought process isn't limited to disease. Any time we're presented with a random scenario in which someone experiences a chance harm, our brains flip the scenario into a lesson to be learned—a way to avoid experiencing the same harm ourselves.

When we offer advice on avoiding random misfortune, we reassure ourselves that we are immune to these kinds of things. We create a "manageable and predictable world," in which we control our personal and professional outcomes. We free ourselves—at least to a degree—from fear of random violence, loss, or other misfortune. Our ability to predict the outcomes of our behaviors is, Lerner wrote, "central to the ability to engage in long-term goal-directed activity."

In essence, we are hardwired to believe that we are in control of our own destiny, at least to a degree. Unable to handle the implications of a random, unjust world, we create stories to explain why bad things happen. And in our stories, those bad things don't happen to *us*. They happen to people who deserve them, at least a little bit.

In other words, we refuse to cede control of our lives to fate.

But what if that also means that we miss out when what appears to be a misfortune instead has an outsized *positive* effect on our lives? What if we get so entrenched in our plans for safety and success that we overlook the role of the unexpected?

SLUMDOG MILLIONAIRE

On a balmy Saturday morning, I unexpectedly found myself wandering the streets of Rio's most drug-ridden *favela*—trying hopelessly to blend in with my khakis and a polo—with no GPS and no idea what to do.

A favela is a term commonly used in Brazil to describe informal, densely populated settlements located near the boundaries of major cities. They typically lack resources like safe housing and clean water, and are often controlled by drug traffickers, gangs, or corrupt, violent police activity. So while I love exploring a variety of cultures and environments—and I can be pretty daring about venturing off the beaten path—favelas are not considered safe places for outsiders.

But I was new to Rio. I had no idea where I was until I landed there by chance.

Just a few months before, after spending the first two years of my career in a Fortune 500 company, I realized that I wasn't cut out for big company life. I'd overheard a conversation with a senior exec and, being as stubborn and self-assured as most twenty-two-year-olds, I interrupted the conversation to share my own perspective.

The exec quickly shut me down.

We only exchanged a few lines, but in that brief conversation, I realized how little I really knew. And I realized I needed to learn more.

So I started looking for job opportunities outside of the company. I thought a smaller organization would operate at a faster pace. In a smaller environment, I would be closer to my colleagues in other departments. I could explore my curiosities and learn by observing others.

Coincidentally a family friend had ties to a small manufacturing company in Brazil that was looking for someone with my skill set. After a short conversation with the hiring manager, I took a week off work to fly to Brazil, interview with the company, and get a feel for life in Rio.

I immediately fell in love with the city and culture. The people of Rio (*Cariocas*, in Portuguese) are fun, warm, and very appreciative of their beautiful beaches. My future co-workers were impressive, and the work aligned with my skills. Even the thought of struggling to learn Portuguese appealed to me.

When I came back to the US and told my boss I was leaving the company, she told me she wasn't surprised. The company made a heartfelt effort to keep me, but the allure of caipirinhas, late night samba, and *pão de queijo* was too enchanting to ignore.

I sold all my belongings and prepared to move to Rio. My suitcases were fully intact—no need for a hairpin patch job—but in many ways, I was just as unsettled as the young girl in Hollywood.

One weekend I had to go into work on a Saturday morning; the office was about forty-five minutes from my apartment, depending on the mode of transportation. Subways and taxis were either too slow or too expensive, so I often took the bus.

That Saturday, I boarded the bus as usual, but I didn't realize that the route changed on weekends—the bus I was on wouldn't stop at my normal location. As soon as I realized what was happening, I got off at the next stop. I figured I was only a twenty-minute walk from my typical stop, so I might as well take the last leg on foot.

I'd barely stepped away from the bus stop when a crack addict stumbled aimlessly toward me, his eyes glazed and his head wobbling.

"*Dineirho?*" he slurred.

"*Não,*" I stammered.

Stepping out of his path, I trudged on, artfully dodging the human feces on the side of the street. Children who had been playing exuberantly paused to stare at me, their dark skin slick and shiny with sweat. I kept walking.

After about ten minutes of walking, I was terrified. I very clearly did not fit in—Jacarezinho residents often lovingly refer to the area as "the Blackest favela in Rio" while I've been referred to as "the whitest guy in Kansas" —and since my phone didn't have GPS, I had very little hope that I would make it to the office.

Frantic, I called my boss. But when she asked where I was, I had no idea what to tell her. "Uh, I see some concrete houses," I stammered. "And a dirt road..."

I took another step forward, scanning the scene for a landmark. When I glanced to my left, I jumped. An older man stood directly beside me, looking at me expectantly.

"*Você está perdido?*" he asked, and I nodded enthusiastically—I *was* lost.

My heart thudded in my chest, and a bead of sweat rolled down my forehead, resting finally on my upper lip.

The man reached for my phone, and I handed it to him. Maybe I shouldn't have, but somehow, I trusted him. And, in truth, I was grateful to be told what to do.

He and my boss, Carol, exchanged a few lines in Portuguese, and he handed the phone back to me.

Carol's voice came through the line. "*Don't move,*" she said. "I'm coming to get you."

I thanked her—the sincerest gratitude I'd expressed since I'd been in Rio and maybe in my entire life—and hung up the phone. I just had to wait it out. Carol was coming to rescue me.

With a tilt of his head, a signal that I should follow him, the man turned and walked to the cart parked on the corner of two dirt roads. Before I could follow him, two men turned the corner, eyeing me with a look that felt menacing, at least in my current terrified state. I scrambled to join the man, who introduced himself as Francisco, in his makeshift corner store.

As I sat on the little stool he offered me, I took in the space. Pinned neatly along the top of the cart were pictures. In one prominent black-and-white photo, a young woman gazed past the camera. Her face was solemn but beautiful, her hair piled neatly on her head. Another photograph featured several bare-chested children in brightly colored shorts. They weren't so different from the kids I'd encountered when I climbed off the bus, except these children were clearly flexing for the camera, not staring blankly at a lost white guy who had no business in their neighborhood.

I didn't know Francisco, but somehow, he felt safe and familiar. In reality, he may have saved my life that day—I very obviously did not fit in and would have made an easy target for anyone with nefarious purposes in mind. I found Francisco's kindness to be remarkable.

Even more remarkable was the wisdom he shared.

"There are a lot of challenges in this community," he said in Portuguese. He glanced at the children playing nearby, his face almost unreadable. "There's a lot of crime and corruption. People don't have enough money."

I nodded. I didn't want to seem overly enthusiastic in my agreement—this was his community, after all—but I could tell he'd thought carefully about the experiences of the favela's citizens, his family included.

As if reading my mind, he pointed toward the pictures I'd noticed when I sat down. "My daughter," he said, pointing to the image of a young girl. "She's a teacher." He smiled, his eyes glistening. Indicating the child next to her, he said, "And my niece is a doctor." As he continued, pointing out each of his family members, he radiated pride. "They all grew up here," he said. "With a little hard work, we can make things better." His voice sounded a little weathered, but his passion was clear. "We have to come together. We have to serve each other."

Before that point, I hadn't thought much about the role business could play in social change. But as Francisco and I talked (or, rather, as Francisco talked and I listened —my Portuguese was elementary at best!), I saw the connection.

Entrepreneurship wasn't just about money. It was about making the world a better place.

As Carol pulled up—a look of relief on her face—Francisco wished me well. I thanked him for his help and for his wisdom, for the lessons I had craved without even knowing they were possible. I climbed into Carol's Fiat, and she drove me to work.

To an onlooker, my day turned out to be relatively ordinary. I'd started with a little hiccup—stepping off the bus at the wrong stop—but everything had turned out fine. It was just another day.

Except it wasn't just another day.

Getting lost in the favela had changed my life, but not in the way many might assume—I wasn't mugged or harassed, even *in the slightest sense*. But that conversation with Francisco changed my life. I knew even then that our conversation had profoundly altered my psyche.

I'd come to Rio to learn. But I never could have predicted how it would happen.

"A MONUMENTAL TANTRUM"

When the young woman strode into the downtown Los Angeles bank, the lunch-rush lines had already begun to form. Like most of us at nineteen or twenty, I imagine, she was impatient—annoyed at having to wait when there was so much life out there to be lived.

Eventually, she reached the teller and presented the check, the last remnant of her New York modeling career and her only resource for paying rent.

"I just need this cashed, please." She fiddled with the beaded chain that connected the pen to the counter and glanced around at the line of customers beside her.

"Do you have an account with us?" the teller asked.

"No," she replied. "I just need it cashed."

"Unfortunately," the teller replied, "we can't cash an out-of-state check if you don't have an account with us."

The teller slid the check back across the counter, and

the young woman's stomach lurched. That check was the difference between staying in Los Angeles and returning to South Africa. With $500, she could afford to stay another month—a lean month, certainly, but another month—and work toward her big break.

"It's from a modeling agency," she insisted. "See," she pointed at the check's header. "You can see here. The check is good."

"I understand, ma'am," the teller said. "But it's our policy."

The young woman shook her head, a hot mixture of anger and desperation churning in her gut. "I don't think you *do* understand! I need this money. If I don't get this cashed—"

"Please lower your voice, ma'am."

"I don't understand why you can't just cash it!" Her voice grew louder and shriller, and somehow the sound focused her. She had no choice—she had to change this teller's mind—so she launched into her most persuasive arguments. The agency was legitimate. It wasn't much money for a downtown LA bank. She needed that money to live. She needed that money to build her career.

Just as she was escalating into a finale of epic proportions, she heard a man's voice behind her. "Excuse me," he said. "Maybe I can help."

The young woman wiped her eyes and turned to find a middle-aged man with thick-coiffed hair and a subtly stylish business suit. Dumbfounded, the young woman just stared.

Turning to the teller, the man asked, "Could you please get the paperwork to open a new account?"

The young woman didn't object, other than to offer a few sniffles, as the man took a stack of forms from the teller and handed them to her.

"You'll need to open an account," he said. "But that's not difficult. If you just fill out these forms, they'll take care of it. You can cash your check and be on your way." He flashed a charming half-smile, the kind it seemed every man in LA had perfected, and she took the forms from him, gave the teller a side-eyed glance, and wandered over to the bank's sitting area to fill them out.

Moments later, the man was at her side again. This time he held a crisp, white business card. "If you're interested," he said, "I'll represent you."

The front of the card read "John Crosby, Talent Scout."

If Crosby hadn't been in the bank that day to witness what some described as a "monumental tantrum," Charlize Theron might have had to return to South Africa.

Instead, less than a year later, that young woman had landed her first Hollywood role. A decade later, she'd won an Oscar.

WHEN CHANCE TAKES YOU

There is tremendous power in taking control of our own lives. If we don't push ourselves toward our goals, we will never reach them. Our success depends on our willingness to take control of and responsibility for our own actions.

However, too often we overestimate our power. Like the office-mates who question whether Deb brought about her own cancer diagnosis, we ignore the role of chance in our lives. We assume that anything truly important—truly life-changing—will be a result of our own choices and actions.

But when we really stop to consider the defining points of our lives, it becomes clear that the most profound shifts contained an element of surprise. A single, unpredictable moment had an outsized and irreversible impact on our lives.

I call those moments *catalysts*, and the primary purpose of this book is to explore their meaning. But this purpose, in and of itself, will not be immediately clear to the reader. After all, stories like Charlize Theron's bank encounter, like my conversation with Francisco, can seem trivial. You've probably read about stories like these before, of coincidences that make us say, "Huh, so *that's* how that happened. Interesting!"

I agree—these stories *are* interesting, and they *do* appear to be coincidences.

But *Luck by Design* is about more than just marveling at life's quirks. These fascinating stories of serendipity—of opportunity crafted from tragedy, of chance conversations that redefined their participants' lives, or of being in the right place at the right time—are not the end point of this book. Rather, these stories provide entry into a fascinating world of social and natural science. In the pages that follow, I'll illustrate how these moments have worked for household names and ordinary people like you and me. But more than that, I use the discoveries of modern psychology, philosophy, natural science, and metaphysics to understand not only *why* these things happen, but, even more fascinating, why we feel compelled to understand them in the way we do, as 'chance' instances rather than the very fabric of life.

In his 2007 book *The Black Swan: The Impact of the Highly Improbable*, Nassim Nicholas Taleb explores the phenomenon of "black swan events," unexpected and unlikely historical moments that shape the world's trajectory.[4] These moments—such as the rise of the internet and 9/11—were unpredictable in both their timing and impact. Yet, as Taleb argues, as soon as we understand the ramifications of events like these, we scramble for an explanation. We can't, as a collective society, process the idea that world-changing events can truly be unpredictable.

But when we reflect on our own lives, we often realize something else: that unexpected moments are very often the catalysts for our most major personal life changes. As Taleb writes, "We are quick to forget that just being alive is an extraordinary piece of good luck, a remote event, a chance occurrence of monstrous proportions."

"I DON'T BELIEVE IN LUCK"

In 2003 Charlize Theron won an Academy Award. She'd appeared in twenty-one films by then, including starring roles in feature films like *Monster* (her Oscar-winning role) and *The Devil's Advocate*. In the twenty years following her Oscar win, she nearly tripled that number, in addition to taking on the role of producer, a role she'd tried on first for the film that won her the film industry's most prestigious award.

But arguably her most important role was not on

screen. As many celebrities before her, Charlize leveraged her fame to do good in the world. She founded and actively participates in the Africa Outreach Project, a nonprofit organization dedicated to increasing educational opportunities, health literacy, and public safety for children in southern Africa. She has been outspoken about the rates of sexual assault and domestic violence in her home country and beyond. She has been recognized by the Red Carpet Advocacy organization, has spoken at the World Economic Forum, and in 2008 was named a United Nations Messenger of Peace.

When she moved to Los Angeles, she was determined to succeed, and she worked hard toward that goal. But would any of it have happened had John Crosby not wandered into that particular bank at that particular time on that particular day?

If you were to map my time in Rio, entering each experience and activity into a Gantt chart, my conversation with Francisco would barely register. I spent over a year in Rio, working, playing, learning, growing, and even dancing...or, at least, trying to dance—my moves are better suited to the American Midwest than to South America. I spoke with Francisco for only twenty minutes.

In that brief time, Francisco forever changed the trajectory of my career. As I reflect on the importance of my time in that favela, I've come to the conclusion that I fell in love with business that day. Not because business can make someone fabulously rich but because business can make the world a fabulously better place.

That concept—that business could uplift and serve communities—had never occurred to me before. But suddenly, like a bolt of lightning, I knew what I had to do. I would return to the US and start my own company, a company dedicated to bolstering positive social change.

I use the metaphor of a lightning bolt here very intentionally. Most of us don't worry about getting struck by lightning. When we offer advice to graduating seniors, we rarely offer tips on how to avoid a chance strike—the idea seems far too random, far too distant, to be of much concern. Just one in 15,300.[5]

But if there were a way to add up all the chance occurrences I experienced that day, I suspect the odds would be similar. No one could have predicted that I would step off the bus at a random stop in Rio, wander a random distance through the favela, and stop—randomly—just a few feet from the man who would change my life. If I tried it again, I think I'd have a better shot at getting struck by lightning.

That's the thing about chance. We can't control it. No matter how much we want to.

What would the world be like if, instead of marveling at the strange coincidences in our everyday lives, we respected those moments' life-changing potential? What if we used them to understand the ways we can—and, as importantly, *cannot*—control the things life throws our way?

In 2005 Oprah interviewed Charlize for *O, The Oprah Magazine*. As Charlize recounted her experience of moving to LA, she attributed the bank story to being in the "right place, right time—luck."[6]

But Oprah pushed back. "I don't believe in luck," she replied.

Whether luck or destiny, coincidences like this aren't once-in-a-million chance occurrences.

They happen often. More often than you might think.

What could the future look like if, instead of trying to explain them away, we embraced them? What if, instead, we recognized that unexpected events play a major role in our lives' trajectory?

What if we embraced our catalysts?

CHAPTER 2
THE MOMENT EVERYTHING CHANGED

"Where were you on 9/11?" Millennials ask one another.

Gen Xers vividly remember the Challenger explosion.

Before that, Boomers recalled the assassinations of both John F. Kennedy and Martin Luther King Jr.

And Sarajevans remember the siege that turned their world upside down.

In the mid-1990s the city had been a hot spot for one of the twentieth century's most devastating human rights crises. The Siege of Sarajevo marked the beginning of what would later be called the Bosnian genocide, a period in which Serbs murdered thousands of Bosniaks—also called Bosnian Muslims—in one of the largest ethnic-cleansing campaigns since World War II.

All told, the siege had lasted 1,425 days—nearly four years. Snipers shot down into the city's thoroughfares from the hilly regions above. Shells were dropped on citizens as they stood in line for water. Bullets were fired through families' windows. By some estimates, more than twelve thousand people died.[1]

A decade later, a young woman walked into a memory research lab in Sarajevo, the city where she grew up. She wasn't sure what kinds of memories she would be asked to share. Casual observers might assume she would be asked about the siege that transformed her home city into a war zone.

Casual observers would be wrong.

Instead, the young woman was given a stack of notecards, each with a different word.

Automobile.
Chair.
Street.
Dog.
Pill.

"Take the first card," the researcher instructed, "and think of a memory you associate with that word. Then write a one-sentence description of that memory at the bottom of the card."

The woman nodded, furrowing her brow at the first word. *Automobile.*

"The memory must be at least one week old," the researcher continued. "If you can't think of a memory for any particular word, you may skip that word."

Picking up a pen from the table, the woman nodded and got to work.

The first two answers were relatively innocuous. *Automobile*—she wrote first about riding into the nearest town with her brother. *Chair*—she recalled the prized seat at the dinner table, the one right next to their father, that both she and her brother had coveted as children.

It was the third memory that carried emotional heft. She stared at the word—*Street*—for several seconds before jotting down a quick description of the time she'd lost a hairpin in the street outside her home.

When she finished, she flipped to the next card.

LIVING IN HISTORY

Why would researchers ask the young woman—and more than 250 other subjects from eight countries around the world—to share memories associated with such mundane terms? In Bosnia, in particular, a country where thousands of civilians had died in a genocide, why not explore the obvious psychological implications of living through something so traumatic?

For psychology researchers, the answer is obvious—to get at the real effects of trauma, researchers can't simply ask participants to talk about difficult things. Humans are notoriously terrible at estimating the effects of any singular event on our mental health, for one thing.[2] For a second, most of us can't recall the minutiae of our everyday lives even a week or two after the fact—do you remember what you wore to work two Tuesdays ago?

Human bias is the third and most important reason psychology researchers don't ask participants to simply explain which events changed their lives. Through decades of studying the intricacies of human psychology, researchers realized that study participants often respond according to what they believe researchers want to hear, which may or may not coincide with what they actually feel.

Over time, social scientists have gotten smarter about their research design. Instead of asking people about their trauma *directly*, they ask them to recall other things that seem completely unrelated to trauma.

If you ask someone about their trauma and they respond by telling you about their trauma, you haven't learned much.

But if you ask people about innocuous things—*Automobile, Chair, Street*—and they respond by telling you about their trauma, you're on to something.

This is precisely why the researchers in Sarajevo asked the young woman to list memories associated with ordinary, unremarkable words. They wanted to see whether everyday memories would prompt a discussion of major world events.

In that room in Sarajevo, the young woman had finished her initial task—each card had a brief handwritten note indicating a memory she associated with the card's keyword.

But the session had only just begun.

Once she finished, the researcher picked up the cards and, one by one, asked the woman to place each memory on a timeline of her life. "As you come up with each date, please verbalize your thoughts," they said. "No matter how trivial they might seem."

This was where the real research happened.

First, the woman talked about riding in the car with her brother, the memory she associated with the *Automo-*

bile cue. She talked next about the chair that she and her brother fought over as children.

Finally, she reached the card that read *Street*.

"That's also in childhood," she said. "And it happened during the war period, when I walked with my friends down the street." She nodded to herself, and her eyes went distant for a moment. "I got the pin from my mom, and it had sentimental value," she continued, "and looking for it, I realized it was gone."

The researcher gave her a sympathetic look and nodded for her to continue.

"I felt sad," she said. "That was in spring."

Without knowing it, the young woman had just demonstrated the exact psychological construct the researchers were exploring—a concept they call the living-in-history effect. The protocol for the study was simple. Researchers asked participants to narrate their thought process as they located their memories in time. They wanted to see whether participants would lean on *public events*—the types of occurrences that are recorded in history books, including genocide and war—as anchors for their more personal memories.

And that's precisely what the young woman did. By connecting the lost hairpin with "the war period," she demonstrated that she'd been "living in history."

This result may seem obvious. When we live through something catastrophic, it seems reasonable to experience that historical event as an important part of our lives. Again and again, the Bosnian participants proved this supposition true—they connected their personal autobiographical memories to those years in the early 1990s when their country transformed into a war zone.

But the study wasn't about Bosnia, in particular. It was about the psychological patterns that occur in all places where major, world-changing, historical events occur. So they gathered participants from several places that fit the bill: Sarajevo, Israel, and, since it was the early 2000s, New York City.

In Israel, the results were the same—people used war to anchor their personal, everyday memories.

But when researchers spoke with people in New York City, a space that had looked very much like a war zone only a few Septembers before, the responses they received were very different.

In Bosnia, participants had tied their experiences to genocide. Israeli participants connected their memories to the army. So the researchers expected New York participants to tie their memories to 9/11.

No one did.

When the Living in History researchers sat down with their data, they faced an interesting analytical problem. They'd come to the project with a hypothesis: that major world events would be tied to everyday lived experiences in the memories of those who lived them.

Their hypothesis was wrong.

In the very epicenter of an event that defined a generation, no participants tied 9/11 to their everyday lived experiences. Less than five years after the devastating event occurred—before ground was broken for a 9/11 monument—the study asked participants to share random memories. None of those memories involved the attack.

The results of the Living in History project forced researchers to rethink the way psychology approaches autobiographical memory, the concept at the heart of the study. Where it was once assumed that these world events profoundly changed our everyday lives, the study made it clear that more was at play.

For the participants in the study, an event that should have shifted the trajectory of their lives…simply…didn't.

It was an outcome no one could have predicted.

SPEAKING OF HYPOTHESES

As the Living in History researchers teach us, it's difficult to predict the outcome of major world events on memory. How do our minds process the fact that, completely by chance, our lives have been flipped upside down by genocide, terrorism, or war? What can living-in-history teach us about the other chance events that turn our lives around?

As I discussed in the previous chapter, we often find ways to blame the victims of things like terminal disease as a way to protect our own psyches from the risks of such devastating, random events. But when *we* become the victims, things look quite different.

Take, for instance, Stephen Hawking. He is known by most for two discrete things.

First, he revolutionized how humans understand the universe. A highly decorated scholar, Hawking reshaped the meaning of matter—and his book *A Brief History of Time* became a global sensation, captivating a broad readership despite its heady concepts.

The British-born scientist grew up in a highly intellectual family, but when he took an interest in mathematics —a field that spoke to his love of certainty—his father balked at the idea. A medical doctor, the elder Hawking expected his son to follow in his footsteps, but Stephen resisted, instead proposing a compromise: he would study both chemistry *and* physics.

But he wouldn't study either with much enthusiasm, at least not initially. Hawking was, perhaps surprisingly, a bit of a slacker during his undergraduate career. While he earned reasonable grades, he never felt challenged—he got bored easily and preferred to focus on social events and the rowing team.

Second, Hawking is known for his disability, the result of a disease that emerged—completely randomly—in his early twenties. Around that time, Hawking began to notice a new clumsiness in himself. He began to stammer and stutter during ordinary conversations, a problem he'd never experienced before. Eventually, the problem became too intrusive to ignore, so he visited his family doctor.

Today, medical professionals estimate that between 90 and 95 percent of ALS cases are "sporadic," meaning that they have no identifiable link to family history or other risk factors. In other words, the vast majority of ALS diagnoses are completely and totally random.

Hawking had to process all of that at only twenty-one years old. And he had something else to process, too—he was given just two years to live.

A terminal diagnosis can, understandably, shatter one's predictions for the future. Having never faced this devastating experience in my own life, my ability to imagine the scenario is based on watching relatives go through the stages of grief following the news. It is, without a doubt, a profoundly destabilizing event—one that could easily dictate how a person chooses to live out their remaining days.

For some, a terminal diagnosis sets them on a path of exploration and discovery. If they've always wanted to see the aurora borealis, they book a trip to Sweden. If they've dreamed of gathering their family for a weeklong getaway, they send the invitations. If they've wanted to go skydiving or Rocky Mountain climbing or bull riding, Tim McGraw tells us, they might make those things happen.

Others, understandably, move through the classic stages of grief: denial, anger, bargaining, and depression before, hopefully, finally landing on acceptance.

In the majority of stories that circulate in our culture, those are the two primary reactions. Both indicate that for those who experience this type of diagnosis, a terminal disease is *the* single chance occurrence most likely to shape their lives—even the most steadfast among us are expected to redefine our trajectories in the face of such an unsettling experience.

Terminal disease—like genocide or terrorism—takes its victims by chance. In Hawking's case, ALS was a random occurrence, a roulette wheel whose ball that happened to land on the student before he'd even finished college. These are the types of chance occurrences we *expect* to change our lives.

But we experience other types of chance occurrences every single day. And, just like terminal diagnoses or terrorist attacks, they have the ability to radically alter our future trajectories.

"THE FABRIC OF DAILY LIFE"

Just like every other day, many chance occurrences took place on September 11, 2001. Most of us are very familiar with one of these events: the World Trade Center's twin towers fell, killing thousands of people who just happened to be in the area.

But that wasn't the only random event that took place that day.

On September 11, 2001, a woman who was searching for work boarded the subway and randomly bumped into an old high school friend whose company happened to be hiring. Someone else accidentally clicked a link on the internet, then another, and another, until they'd lost their life's savings to a sophisticated scammer. A hiker reached the summit of a mountain peak and realized, as he took in the breathtaking view, that he needed to get help for his alcoholism.

Each of these events is profoundly life-changing. But we often overlook their causes, the tiny, seemingly insignificant moments like boarding a subway car, searching the internet, or going for a hike. Moments like these are far from the type of event we expect to change our lives.

As a result, we assume that the important events will be *obviously* important—the life-changing occurrences will be *obviously* life-changing. We predict which events matter based on which events have mattered in the past, based on our singular, imperfect observations.

In reality, it's impossible to predict which chance experience will bend the pipeline of our lives' trajectories. Sometimes, the life-changing occurrence is a major world event—certainly many people's lives were impacted by 9/11, just as the young Bosnian woman's life was altered by genocide and war.

But, as the Living in History researchers concluded, major world events don't always shape our lives the way we expect. Those researchers acknowledge that these major, world-changing events *produce the necessary elements* to shape our perspectives on life. And yet, simply living through a major event isn't enough to embed it into our everyday memories.

When the researchers looked at the data they'd collected from participants who *did* incorporate historical events into their everyday memories, they found one thing in common—those events didn't just happen *to* them. The events also, they note, "produced dramatic, *enduring* changes *in the fabric of daily life.*"[3]

The events were *extraordinary*, but it was their influence on the *ordinary* that made them so life-changing.

Catalysts are all about chance—the random moments that change our lives forever—but chance isn't enough. As the Living in History researchers concluded, chance only introduces disturbance into our lives. It's what comes next that matters—it's how those events interact with our everyday habits and thought patterns, and the actions we take afterwards.

ANOTHER RANDOM OCCURRENCE

When Hawking received his diagnosis, he sank into a deep depression. He'd dreamed of becoming a professor. Now, as far as he was concerned, that plan was off the table. He didn't have much interest in experiencing new things. His life, he believed, was over.

He was wrong.

Sometime after his diagnosis, he was reunited with a woman he'd met through a family friend. Jane Wilde was smitten with Hawking and, to his shock, she remained interested in him even when he revealed his prognosis.

The reunion gave him new life. At the time, getting married required a job. If he wanted to marry Jane—and he very much did—he needed to get to work. So, motivated by a chance-meeting-turned-intention, Hawking returned to school, completed his PhD, and landed a research fellowship at Cambridge.

The rest is history.

Decades later, Larry King would ask Hawking how the disease impacted his work. Hawking replied with the linguistic equivalent of a shrug. The disease didn't really factor into his life's work, he replied, other than getting him out of classroom teaching and boring meetings. As he explained, he didn't really like to think about it—there were more important things on his plate.

When King turned the discussion to Jane, on the other hand, Hawking's response was quite different. "The engagement changed my life," he said. "It gave me something to live for."

THE PRIZE BIRD

Imagine you're a turkey.

Like all turkeys, you were born suspicious—new things are not to be trusted. You're constantly on alert for anything that seems out of the ordinary. With that level of diligence, you're bound to see any life-changing events coming from miles away.

Fortunately, your life is more or less the same with each passing day. You wake up in the same coop every morning when your farmer scatters feed on the ground outside. Along with your yard-mates, you march outside for breakfast. The rest of the day is spent rooting around in the dirt. Maybe, like Stephen Hawking, you stumble into a mate. If something seems out of place, you ruffle your feathers.

For as long as you can remember, this has been your life—your second birthday was the same as your first, day 927 the same as day 42.[4] The coop is reliable shelter; the farmer provides reliable food. This, you think, must be what life *is*. Safe. Easy. Predictable.

And you've got the data to prove it!

Just as the scientific method prescribes, you've spent 1,000 days learning by observation. In qualitative psychology research, this effect is called saturation. Once you've seen the same thing over and over and over again, you can be sure the pattern is important. The correlation is as neat and tidy as it gets: as time ticks on, so too does your security. You've proven—with statistical significance—that life is good.

Then comes day 1,001.

That day is the third Wednesday in November. You emerge from your coop to find that you have not, in fact, been fed. *Just an oversight*, you think. *Nothing so mundane could signal anything terribly important.*

In a way, you're right—the missed feeding is *not* the thing that will change your life.

In another, you're terribly wrong. The thing that will change your life—or, rather, end it—is the slow forward movement of time as it rolls forward to Thanksgiving. The missing meal didn't signal a change in your feeding schedule, or, at least, that wasn't the most important thing it signaled.

It signaled, in reality, something much more profound. Your data wasn't wrong, per se. You simply lacked context.

You thought anything large enough to change your life would be clearly and obviously visible. You could spot it from miles away. Just as the captain of the Titanic said in 1907, five years before the ship sank, killing 1,500 people and changing the way we understand safety on passenger ships, you might think, "I never saw a wreck and never have been wrecked nor was I ever in any predicament that threatened to end in disaster of any sort."[5]

But past experience falls short of predicting future experience. What we've seen before is just that—what we've seen before. What's still to come is a mystery.

Maybe you realize that as the farmer grabs you by the neck and drags you to the tree stump behind the barn.

INVITATIONS AND PROTOTYPES

I don't blame Thanksgiving turkeys for lacking a larger context in which to see their own lives. For most of us—turkeys and humans alike—we're too busy living our lives to see the bigger picture.

We wake up. Eat breakfast. Go to work. Play with our kids. Sleep. Rinse and repeat.

The habits that make up our lives very often begin in childhood. We grow up watching people like parents, teachers, and friends, learning all the basic building blocks of a good life—we inherit their interpretations of what it means to put in a good day's work, what it means to love your family, and what it means to find occasional rest and enjoyment.

As a young adult, I was no exception.

I'd spent my childhood watching my parents, absorbing the patterns I saw from those around me. That included my father's habits. Like Stephen Hawking's father, mine also expected that I would follow in his foot-steps, just as he had followed in his own father's. He was a military-officer-turned-government-worker (and every-thing that entails), and I just...wasn't. For my family, the goal of work and money centered on one, clear objective: stability.

There's nothing inherently wrong about my father's approach—it's understandable to want the safety of a biweekly paycheck, quality medical insurance, and the ability to put food on the table every night.

As I grew up—watching, observing, learning, internal-izing—I stumbled on something that piqued my curiosity.

I found microbiology through a simple handwashing experiment in elementary school. I was fascinated by the things we can't see and how they impact us in our lives, and I carried that interest into college. Having long ago accepted my marching orders—*steady paycheck or military* —I saw only a few prescribed paths: I could go to medical school. I could go to graduate school and train to work in a lab. Or I could join the military.

Enter my shaggy-haired, gangly-limbed, pot-smoking fraternity brother who also happened to be extremely, wildly, off-the-charts intelligent.

"Hey," he said one day, appearing in my doorway. He leaned against the doorframe with a hint of a smile at the corner of his mouth. "I have an idea. But I need your help."

I turned down the volume on *Family Guy*, and he plopped down next to me on the ratty, decades-old couch parked in the corner of my room.

A business major, he'd heard about a pitch competition that was being hosted by the college of business. The idea was to encourage aspiring entrepreneurs to pitch their idea for a new product or service, then award the winner some seed money to get their business off the ground.

He wanted me to partner with him to pitch a product at the competition.

I really liked the guy, but, career-wise, we had very little in common...which is the nice way of saying that I almost laughed him out of the room. Something like that —a pitch competition for *entrepreneurs*—a word I could barely pronounce—wasn't anywhere on my radar. I had no idea what a value proposition was, and I'd never put together a contract. I can say that I'd never even thought about the fact that money needs to exchange hands for businesses, and the world, to work.

Simply put—the thought of being an entrepreneur had never crossed my mind.

I'm sure he saw resistance written all over my face, so he stopped me before I could protest. "I don't need you to do anything for the business side," he said. "I just need you to present the idea. You can speak in front of people. You're good at pitching things."

It was a strange assertion, given that he'd only heard me speak in situations with much lower stakes—fraternity meetings and maybe a class presentation or two.

But my bigger concern was that I knew *literally nothing* about business.

"Listen," he said when I expressed my concerns, "I'll write the business plan. I just need you to get in front of the judges and 'wow' them so we can win this money."

If there's one thing that gets a college student's attention, it's money...or food...or maybe beer. In any case, money could buy all the trappings of an amazing night of partying.

"How much are we talking about?" I asked.

"Dude," he said, in that stoner stereotype that was, in this case, accurate. "It's like...$10,000."

Up to that point I had spent three years working in a professor's research lab on campus. My total income from that job amounted to less than the prize for a single speech.

I was in.

The concept we would be pitching was as simple as it was brilliant. My fraternity brother worked at Papa Johns, where the back of the restaurant looked something like the counter at Subway or Chipotle. Before each shift, ingredients were prepped and dumped into small, rectangular bins lined up in a pizza assembly line. To make a pizza, workers lay out the dough, spread sauce on it, then reach into the bins for toppings. They grab a handful of sausage, scatter it across the pie, a handful of green peppers, grabbed and scattered, a handful of black olives, and so on until your pizza is ready, just the way you like it.

But as the line cooks grabbed and scattered, grabbed and scattered, grabbed and scattered, ingredients would spill over the sides of the bins, contaminating toppings with other toppings. So a lot of people opened their large pepperoni pizza to find a few stray onions or a crumble of sausage (bonus!).

The problem is, some people don't like green pepper on their pizza.

Others are allergic to dairy.

And a vegetarian definitely won't see that sprinkle of sausage as a bonus.

Our solution? Design and sell dividers that could be inserted between the bins.

Prior to the pitch, we made a few dividers and installed them in his restaurant, and then videotaped a worker making pizzas. The results were clear. As the worker assembled the pies—grabbing and scattering and grabbing and scattering—you could actually see the ingredients stacking up against the dividers.

When we got in front of the judges and showed the video as part of our pitch, one of them actually said, "Wait a second. Why doesn't this already exist?"

The idea was a true no-brainer.

When the judges handed us our giant novelty check, we both grinned from ear to ear. We'd created a product, and a panel of experts thought it merited a sizable investment. It felt amazing.

Before my friend invited me to join his pitch competition team, my entire future had been planned out. I would go to school—possibly long enough to earn a graduate degree—and then I would interview with companies in my chosen field. I would get a job with a steady paycheck. I would go to work every day. I would watch TV. I would sleep. Rinse and repeat. Just another happy turkey.

It wasn't particularly exciting, but it was what I knew.

It was, I believed, predictable.

But when my friend plopped down on my couch to invite me to join a pitch competition, my life changed. Before that moment, I'd never seen entrepreneurship as an option. That moment sent me down a path that would show me my potential future in business. I was like an old tree that had sprouted a new branch, or a hiker who wanders along the Appalachian Trail to find a path that seems to have appeared out of nowhere.

That moment had opened my mind to a new future— one I'd never imagined—where business was a possible career path.

His invitation was a catalyst.

I didn't realize it then. But if that conversation had never happened, I don't think I'd be where I am today.

Like the Thanksgiving turkey, I would have used my past
—and my parents' pasts, and their parents' past—to
determine my future. I would have kept on keeping on,
living the predetermined plan that had been set for me
from birth.

Like that turkey, I lacked context. I assumed that every
day should be more or less the same, that stability and
routine were simply the way things should be done. I'd
seen it in my parents for my entire life, each day adding to
my certainty that this was simply the way life was.

I'd never known any different.

The past was predictable, so I assumed the future was,
too. Until one moment, something happened. It wasn't a
terminal diagnosis or a genocide. It wasn't a terrorist
attack or a farmer with an axe.

It was just a guy standing in my doorway.

THE TROUBLE WITH COMMON SENSE

What would my life be like if my fraternity brother had
asked someone else to pitch his idea, or simply given up
because he wasn't a confident speaker?

If John Crosby hadn't been in that Los Angeles bank,
would we know who Charlize Theron is?

What if Stephen Hawking hadn't bumped into his
wife, a woman he barely knew? Would we know as much
about the universe?

Those moments have two things in common. First,
they're completely unpredictable. Second, they have an
unanticipated, outsized effect on our lives.

As a college student, I had no idea what kinds of

things would shape my life, but I certainly didn't expect a casual chat to reshape my entire career trajectory. Common sense tells us that those kinds of divergences are more likely to occur during a one-on-one advising session with a professor or a career-oriented campus activity.

Common sense is wrong.

I suspect that most people would have discouraged Charlize from her epic tantrum. After all, a meltdown in a public space doesn't usually lead to anything positive. As common sense tells us, it's not a tantrum in a bank that launches an acting career—it's an audition.

Common sense is wrong.

And then there's Stephen Hawking. When Hawking was diagnosed with ALS, he was certain that his life was quite literally over. Common sense supports this assumption. On television and in film, terminal diagnoses are almost always the primary driver of a character's story—the moment when things either spiral downward toward demise or, in the more saccharine genres, turn unpredictably uplifting, cruising the audience toward a tearful, bittersweet ending. This pattern, thanks to our common cultural stories, has also become common sense.

But common sense is wrong.

In fact, when it comes to catalysts, common sense may be wrong as often as it's right—when we look back at our months and years of regular, barnyard feedings, we see only steady, reliable nourishment and a warm, safe place to sleep.

When we envision our futures—a form of prediction —we do so from a particular set of data. We compile a set of mental statistics from the billions of moments that make up our lives. But the questions we ask are all wrong.

What events have changed my life in the past?

What events have changed others' lives in the past?

What life-changing events have I seen or read about in the news, in history books, on television, and in all of the other highly predictable stories we tell ourselves about life?

We base our predictions for the future on the events we've observed in the past.

And so, as Nassim Taleb notes, we come to the very understandable conclusion that by looking at the past, we can predict the future. But there's a problem, one that the Living in History project unintentionally uncovered during their months-long research project: we can't predict the future.

So why do we assume our past experiences can?

THE ROUND-TRIP FALLACY

If we assume that only "major" events can change our lives—events like the Bosnian genocide or 9/11—then we necessarily believe that life-changing events will be huge and obvious. If they're major world events, we'll see the commentary on social media. If they're more personal, we're learn about them from our doctor, lawyer, or boss, or spouse.

Life-changing events, common sense tells us, are not subtle.

Taleb calls this assumption the "round-trip fallacy." If we were to observe the turkey for one thousand days, we might assert that "there is *no evidence* of the possibility of large [unpredictable] events." The conclusion *seems* rational—common sense, even.

But many confuse that statement with a slightly different one—those observers may use the strong pattern of evidence to *rule out* large, unpredictable events. Except, as Taleb points out, evidence of a repeating pattern in our lives is *not* evidence that the pattern will repeat indefinitely.

This fallacy, he writes, is an effect of hindsight. By telling ourselves a story about our past observations, we attempt to reverse engineer a predictable world. The problem with the round-trip fallacy, Taleb argues, is that our reverse-engineered datasets can actually be harmful.

If the turkey had predicted what was to come, perhaps he could have escaped. Instead, seeing only good days ahead, he rested, fat and happy in his coop on the Tuesday evening before Thanksgiving.

Assuming that the major turning points in our lives look like a big audition or a terrorist attack or a terminal diagnosis or an exciting first date means that we keep waiting for our catalysts—the random moments that have an outsized impact on our lives. We think we'll know them when we see them.

But how many catalysts have passed us by because we thought they would look like something magnificent or terrifying? How many tiny, random events could have changed our lives if only we were open to them?

Which event is more likely to change a person's life: a terminal diagnosis or a chance interaction with a stranger?

In Hawking's case, if we were asked to guess which

event would redefine his life, most of us would have guessed wrong.

But, of course, Hawking was no turkey.

He said as much in his best-selling book *A Brief History of Time*: "No matter how many times the results of experiments agree with some theory," he wrote, "you can never be sure that the next time the result will not contradict the theory."

Hawking was a theoretical physicist, so when he wanted to understand something, he observed it closely, considering all the possible angles and every bit of available context. But observation is only part of any careful consideration of the universe. To really understand how the universe works, Hawking taught, we need to understand how all the myriad pieces work together.

That's true of catalysts, too. When we look for them, we find them everywhere. But that only tells us that they exist—simple observation falls woefully short of telling us what to do when we experience one.

We have to put on lenses of biology, biochemistry, physics, and psychology and explore catalysts as Hawking would—from every angle. We have to see them not as flukes, but as the very fabric of life itself.

CHAPTER 3
YOU POKE THE BEAR

celand is otherworldly. Quaint villages are nestled among untouched wilderness. Beams of oddly colorful light paint the sky in bright blues and greens. Glaciers tower on the horizon, their icy edges glistening in the sun. Volcanic peaks rise dramatically from the earth, creating a rugged and raw backdrop that speaks of the country's fiery origins. There are black sand beaches, steaming geysers, and fleeting rainbows sketched by the ethereal mists of the hot springs.

But at that moment, I wasn't looking at the gorgeous scenery.

I was looking at a tube of Chapstick.

I'd traveled to Reykjavik with my longtime mentor, a former professor of mine who had become like a second father to me. Over the years, we've traveled to China, Portugal, Spain, and Dubai. Each of those trips was special...but nothing could compare to what happened in Iceland.

When you visit Iceland, the Blue Lagoon is an obligatory destination. It's the most popular tourist spot in the country, home to what they call a geothermal spa—a hot spring that's so rich with minerals that the water takes on an ethereal, glowing, milky white-blue tint that radiates energy. It was as breathtaking and relaxing as we'd been promised.

As we exited through the Blue Lagoon's obligatory gift shop, I glanced around for a souvenir for my girlfriend of eighteen months. They had postcards, of course, and some relatively generic jewelry. There were thick, fluffy towels and heavy robes. But as I wandered through the store searching for the perfect gift, my attention landed on the health and wellness section.

Since the Blue Lagoon is primarily a spa—and since its claim to fame is its mineral-rich water—I knew right away what I wanted to purchase for her.

A tube of Icelandic Chapstick.

Satisfied that I'd landed on just the right gift, I marched the little tube up to the register to pay, my mind already looking ahead to the evening's festivities.

"Find anything good?" my mentor asked, joining me in line.

I turned to him. "Yeah, I think so," I said. I shifted my potential purchases in my hands, first holding up a keychain I picked up for my nephew followed by a post-card I planned to mail home to my mom. Finally, I held up the Chapstick. "And I thought this was kinda cool."

"Huh..." he said. "For...?"

"Oh, for my girlfriend," I replied.

He laughed as though he thought I was making a joke. "You can't get your girlfriend Chapstick!"

I'd known him for years at that point, long enough to know that he was never judgmental. He didn't even offer advice most of the time. Typically, our conversations were packed with positivity and support—he's one of my biggest cheerleaders—and he would spend most of his time just listening and asking questions.

So, surprised by his reaction to something I felt so confident about, I pushed back. "But it's expensive Chapstick," I countered. "It's made with Icelandic minerals."

He raised his eyebrows and shook his head, just a tiny movement, subtle enough that if I didn't know him well, I might have missed it. "Well, unless you're planning to break up with her, you'd better get her something other than Chapstick."

I wasn't planning to break up with her. In fact, the thought hadn't even crossed my mind. Back home, things were good. She and I never fought. We loved each other's families. We'd even survived the transition to long-distance dating when we both left Tucson—me for work in Philadelphia, and her for a new opportunity in Phoenix.

I had no complaints about our relationship.

His comment caught me off guard, but I trust him implicitly, so I asked him what he meant.

"I mean..." he said, looking me straight in the eye. "Really? You don't think you should get something more meaningful?"

It was an interesting observation. I could see what he was saying, but it was so unexpected, I couldn't process it. I felt as satisfied with my relationship as I did with my gift.

So as grateful as I was for his advice, I wasn't particularly interested in changing things up.

He didn't press the issue. By then, we'd reached the front of the gift shop line, so I dropped my items—including the Chapstick—onto the counter and greeted the cashier, the conversation reaching a natural conclusion. As we headed back to the hotel, we transitioned seamlessly into other topics, and by the end of the night, I'd nearly forgotten about his comment.

Nearly.

But not completely.

Just a couple of days later, we boarded a nine-hour flight. And on that flight, I found his words rattling around in my head.

Unless you're planning to break up with her...

The more I thought about it, the more prescient it seemed. Maybe, I realized, this wasn't a *great* relationship. It was good, but maybe it was just good enough to keep me from looking for something amazing.

Maybe I needed to do something different.

By the time my plane landed in San Francisco, I knew what I had to do. My girlfriend had plans to stay with me for the weekend, but I called them off. We'd been completely happy. But that tube of Chapstick—or, more specifically, my mentor's comments about it—made me realize that things weren't as good as I'd assumed.

There was nothing particularly wrong with the relationship.

But it wasn't the right relationship for me, either.

A tube of Icelandic Chapstick made me realize that I

had a choice to make—I could remain comfortable but unfulfilled, or I could embrace the unknown.

In the aftermath of the breakup, there was no emotional tempest to navigate; rather, a newfound clarity settled in. The aftermath of that pivotal conversation had left me more open, more attuned to opportunities I might have dismissed before. That little tube of Chapstick was like the key to a complex machine. When I picked it up at the gift shop, it set off a chain reaction—the Chapstick moved my mentor to offer advice, my mentor's advice shook my mind out of its complacency, my new perspective gave me clarity, and, finally, I broke up with my girlfriend.

That was that.

By that point, the holidays were nearly upon us. Soon October had turned to November and December to a new year. Life went on, and so did I.

But in the first few weeks of 2017, I noticed something.

Or, rather, someone.

I'd known Kelsey for years. We ran in the same social circles, and we had a stable friendship, but I'd never thought of her as anything more. Looking back, I'd never really made space for her to be anything more.

That January, we went on our first date.

Ten months later, we were engaged.

Four more years passed, and our beautiful daughter was born.

It's not that a tube of Chapstick *caused* my marriage— my family—necessarily. But without that tube of Chapstick, things might look very different. And yet, a tube of Chapstick seems completely insignificant.

In a way, that's the point.

FROM CHAPSTICK TO CHILD

What can a mundane purchase in an Icelandic gift shop teach us about catalysts? The answer is both simple and complex.

By definition, a tube of Chapstick cannot be a catalyst —it's an item, not a moment, and in and of itself, it's unlikely to have an outsized impact on our lives. The check Charlize Theron set out to cash is not a catalyst. Neither was the farmer's axe or the pitch competition's giant novelty check. And yet, the presence of these tiny items can—and has—set into motion life-changing moments, moments that demonstrate how the intricate relationship between fate, choice, and the unexpected can carve out the most monumental journeys of our lives.

The profound life changes that chain out from such brief moments make sense—but only in hindsight. Looking back on our lives, we can trace the many links in the chain that lead from a single moment to a major life shift. We can manufacture explanations for why and how these things play out the way they do.

But, by definition, we cannot predict these occurrences. Even the expert social scientists from chapter 2 couldn't predict which things will change our lives and which won't. Sometimes a tube of Chapstick sets a new life trajectory in motion when 9/11 couldn't.

If I had recognized the meaning of that lip balm in the moment, I doubt I would have purchased it. I probably wouldn't have even picked it up. Yet, buying that tube of

Chapstick was one of the most serendipitous decisions of my life, because it set off a sequence of events that made my life what it is today.

That item was the gift shop equivalent of a tiny pebble creating ripples that touch distant shores. That tube of Chapstick was a reminder that we are all part of larger systems, influenced—often invisibly—by connections that extend beyond our immediate awareness.

In pop science, this is often explained through the proverbial notion of the butterfly effect—a concept that asks us to consider whether a butterfly flapping its wings in Ohio can cause a typhoon in Fukushima.

While most scientists agree that this precise scenario is not possible, the concept of the butterfly effect offers a helpful illustration of complex systems theory, a multidisciplinary framework that seeks to explain the behavior of intricate, interrelated systems, each made up of its own interlocking systems. Like cogs in a machine, the individual components of our lives—from our skin and nails to our social roles and environmental interactions—are all part of systems that connect us with others.

That tube of Chapstick was a connection point that set an entire machine in motion. My life is different—*better*—for it.

And the same machine that changed my life in that instant is working in yours as you read this.

MRS. MORTON'S SYSTEM

The first Chapstick was created in the 1880s, but it looked considerably different from the balm we know and love today. A simple tube wrapped in foil, the product was created by a physician and marketed as the ultimate lip balm. There was only one problem.

That original Chapstick looked like a very small candle. And, as such, it didn't seem to fit in with the other items that lived in people's medicine cabinets—pill bottles, tubs of cream, round cardboard boxes of powder, shaving brushes, and so on.

So people didn't know what to do with it.

Discouraged by his product's lack of sales, the original inventor sold the rights to his friend John Morton. In today's dollars, the selling price was around $150. It was a great deal for Mr. Morton—more amazing than either of them knew—but just as the original creator hadn't know how to market the product, neither did Morton.

After several failed attempts, Morton was ready to toss the idea aside and move on to his next venture.

Then, Mrs. Morton stepped in.

She melted down the waxy product and poured it into metal tubes. With its new look, the product suddenly made sense to the mass market. It was like lipstick, but pharmaceutical. Now, potential customers had a frame of reference for the product. Now, they knew what it was for.

With Mrs. Morton's input, the company went from a business that was failing so badly the owners couldn't unload it fast enough to one of the most recognizable brands in the international health and beauty market. It was a change that the original owner couldn't have predicted (otherwise, I suspect he would have kept a tight hold on his company!), and one that allowed Chapstick to weather economic downturn after economic downturn while maintaining a consistently healthy profit margin.

The recipe has changed since Mrs. Morton's 1912 intervention—you'll be relieved to learn that today's Chapstick contains zero earwax, unlike the original formula. When plastic packaging came into vogue, the metal tube was replaced. And a new mechanism—a threaded bar that runs up the center of the balm—was added years later to make the product easier to dispense.

Each of these changes, from the formula to the packaging to the distribution, pricing, and sales, are based on multiple systems, each of which layers into every other system to create something deceptively complex.

Even our day-to-day use of the product is a system—when a user twists the bottom of the tube, the threaded bar catches an internal groove, moving it upwards like a bolt into a nut. One movement leads to another, which leads to another. The waxy substance that emerges as a result is about half white petrolatum. The other half contains recognizable substances like paraffin and alcohol as well as chemical compounds like isopropyl myristate and octyldodecanol.

That last ingredient, octyldodecanol, is technically an inactive ingredient, but it's key to the product's value. Octyldodecanol functions as an emulsifier in many health and beauty products, helping to create a pleasant texture. It's what gives Chapstick that silky feeling, so it slides across your lips in a way that lower-quality products do not.

If we break down octyldodecanol into its simplest parts, the compound is a long-chain fatty alcohol, essentially the chemical version of beads linked together in a long chain. Some of the beads are attracted to water. Others are repelled. The contrast is what helps to stabilize products like Chapstick.

That contrast—and thus octyldodecanol's effectiveness—is created by the precise chemical make-up of the compound. It includes eighteen carbon atoms, thirty-eight hydrogen atoms, and a single atom of oxygen, compounds that are also found in human cells.

In fact, long-chain fatty alcohols are a natural component of lipids—aka fats—that are found in various tissues and cells throughout the body. These fatty alcohols are involved in various physiological processes and play important roles in maintaining the structure and function of cell membranes, as well as contributing to the overall health of the skin and other tissues.

In other words, Chapstick's chemical make-up is so effective because it replicates a tiny part of our physiology. It mimics the natural systems at play in keeping our skin soft and hydrated, allowing it to seamlessly incorporate itself into our body's chemistry.

Thanks to its small size, the product also easily integrates into our daily lives, as we tuck it into our pockets, backpacks, and purses.

And due to Mrs. Morton's reimagining of the product —from the medical branding proposed by the original creator to a health and beauty product that felt right at home next to tubes of lipstick—Chapstick also feels right at home within the economy of consumer-facing brands.

Where the product *doesn't* fit well is in the cup holder of a hot car. Ask me how I know.

Beyond the goopy mess that results when Chapstick is exposed to heat, there's a lesson to be had in the way the product reacts to its environment. It's the same lesson we can draw from its ability to integrate into our body chemistry, into our pockets—and therefore, into our lives—and into the consumer products market.

Systems that interact with their environments are called *open systems*. Open systems exchange matter and energy with their environments (which, of course, are also systems). When the hot sun melts your Chapstick, that product has been affected by its environment. And when you apply Chapstick to your lips, that product has affected its environment, by helping your lips stay smooth and hydrated. That's the very definition of an open system.[1]

While the health and beauty aisle offers plenty of examples of open systems, the open system we most frequently interact with isn't Chapstick—it's *us*.

Humans, like Chapstick, are an open system. When our bodies experience different types of external influences—heat and pressure, as well as the food we eat, the water we drink, the sunlight on our faces—they react accordingly. We sweat from the heat, our muscles ache from prolonged pressure, we create energy from food, and so on.

It all seems incredibly predictable.

But even though we can often predict the cause and effect of various situations—for instance, we know the delectable smells of a delicious meal make our mouths water—open systems are inherently *un*predictable. They constantly interact with their environments, which are, themselves, open systems.

Chapstick seems predictable.

But if a mistake at the production plant caused the octyldodecanol to be absent from Chapstick, the result would feel more like rubbing a candle against your lips.

If the threaded bar on your tube snaps, the product won't come out.

If you leave the cap off, the product will dry out.

We know how Chapstick works to the extent that we know how its *environment* works. But as much as humans try to control our environments, most of us realize it's a losing battle.

Once in a while, your Chapstick is going to melt.

Once in a while, your mentor is going to ask an innocent question.

Once in a while, something will change that's outside of your control, and that change will throw off the predictability of your system.

The bus route will change, and a system that used to take you to work will drop you in a favela. Your meniscus will silently, imperceptibly wear down, and the talent that promised you a professional dance career will be worthless. Something lurking in your DNA will rear its head in a way that nobody really understands, your gait will turn clumsy, and you'll be given two years to live.

Or, maybe, someone buys a bullet.

"KO KO RI KO"

What are you wearing?

A T-shirt? A pair of sweatpants? A tank top?

If you're wearing something made of jersey—that thin,

stretchy cotton or wool fabric that's ubiquitous in casual clothing—you're not alone. By some estimates, 95 percent of Americans own a T-shirt, and most of us own more than one (who doesn't love a free giveaway?!).

In 1883, the year Gabrielle was born, it was unheard of to wear jersey as anything other than men's underwear.

I don't envy people of that time—jersey is soft, breathable, and designed to move with our bodies. It's one of the most versatile textiles available today, and its popularity is only growing.

But in the early twentieth century, it simply wasn't on the radar of the fashion community. Designers didn't stock it. Fabric stores didn't market it. Consumers didn't think about it.

A couple of years earlier, Gabrielle had opened her first boutique, a small but chic storefront in the heart of Paris. She'd always led an active lifestyle, so she had long designed her own clothing, often repurposing men's sportswear—she liked the simple shapes and colors, and she found that the fabric allowed her to move more easily.

While she had a few loyal customers, the business was small, just a tiny space on the ground floor of the flat where she lived with her boyfriend.

Then, on a visit to Sarajevo, Archduke Ferdinand was assassinated.[2] One bullet, fired from one gun, struck the presumptive heir of Austria-Hungary, and the entire world went off-kilter.

Thousands of men from around the world died in the trenches. Meanwhile, Paris exploded into a war zone. Like many of the people around her, Gabrielle fled the area, landing in the small French town of Deauville. The scrappy entrepreneur was determined to maintain her shop's momentum, but there was one problem.

There was no fabric.

War efforts demanded that all textile manufacturers turn their focus to producing materials for uniforms, leaving very few options for women's fashion.

At the same time, the population of women in the workforce grew exponentially, as women took over the jobs men had left behind.

For most designers, these unexpected turns were a death knell—they had no fabric to create their lines, and even if they had, the rigid, immovable designs of the time were ill-suited to the more active lifestyles French women were suddenly engaged in.

In what must have felt like an instant, the system of global politics had tipped on its side, unsettling the worlds' social systems, manufacturing systems, and even systems of thought.

The shift was devastating for some.

It was perfect for Gabrielle.

When she entered the fabric store, she found only men's jersey, a nightmare for most designers but an opportunity for her.

She went to work designing her now-signature menswear-inspired apparel, and, by the end of the war, she'd built an empire. She almost single-handedly introduced pants to women's fashion.[3] She would later credit World War I for launching her business in earnest.

In other words, you're wearing that jersey T-shirt because, somewhere, in 1914, an assassin bought a bullet.

But, of course, it's not as simple as that. Long before

the war prompted Gabrielle to introduce jersey to the masses—a catalyst, to be sure—she'd experienced multiple other systemic upsets.

Born in a "hospice for the poor," Gabrielle was effectively an orphan. Her mother had died when she was a child, and her father abandoned her and her siblings shortly after. The social system of the time—and, in many ways, still today—meant that orphans had very few options, but she survived, no doubt learning resourcefulness from her vulnerability to her environment.

She received a scholarship to attend a religious school at Notre Dame, but because her parents were not paying her way, she experienced the school very differently from her classmates. Namely, she had to work.

At eighteen years old, she learned to make women's hats, the skill that would initially launch her fashion career.

If her mother hadn't died, perhaps her father wouldn't have left.

If her father hadn't left, she certainly wouldn't have been raised an orphan.

If she hadn't been raised an orphan, she might not have attended the school.

If she hadn't attended the school—if she hadn't been required to work as part of her tuition—she might not have learned to make hats.

And if she hadn't learned to make hats, she couldn't have laid the foundation for her fashion empire.

Around that time, she also brought in extra money singing at a café. Her name, then, was Gabrielle. But her signature songs included "*Ko Ko Ri Ko*" and "*Qui qu'a vu Coco dans l'Trocadéro.*" "Coco" was the common thread.

If not for the popularity of these songs in French culture, we might know her as Gabrielle Chanel. But she was a strong singer with an eye for personal branding. She would establish one of the strongest, most iconic brands in fashion and take the throne as one of the wealthiest female entrepreneurs in history.

And, because she picked up a little extra money singing in that café, she quite literally made a name for herself.

Today, we know her as Coco Chanel.

FEEDBACK LOOPS

In the case of Coco Chanel, one catalyst led to the next which led to the next, and the next, and the next. Our view, in hindsight, is of a relatively linear trajectory—a straight line from rags to riches.

That may be how Coco would have described her life. But for most of us, growth isn't so simple. We launch forward, then step back, crawl just a few feet ahead, then fall off a cliff, only to discover a ladder leading us somewhere new. There's a constant push and pull as one force in our lives gives way to an opposing force, a swing rocking back and forth between progress and what we perceive to be decline.

In many ways, this experience makes sense—it's at the very core of our human biology.

Imagine yourself somewhere very cold. If the temperature drops low enough, your body's internal thermostat will sense the drop in temperature. Since our bodies are open systems—meaning that our bodies interact with our environments—the cold around you will trigger a shift in your brain, which will send a signal to your muscles, triggering a shivering response.

The quick, involuntary muscle twitches require energy, and, as they occur, they release some heat. This helps warm you up. As your body struggles to come back to a sustainable temperature, your internal systems—including your brain—will process the return to normal. You'll stop shivering.

This sequence of events—in which a stimulus prompts a systemic change that prompts a counteraction—is called a negative feedback loop. Negative feedback loops appear to be stable, but they inevitably progress toward a breakdown of the system.

Shivering regulates our body temperature, but only to a point. Humans can and do freeze to death. The brain triggers the shivering response, which releases heat, signaling back to the brain, but with each exchange, the effect grows weaker until, eventually, it ceases to function at all.

This progression toward entropy—what Ilya Prigogine called "the arrow of time"—captures the inescapable truth that, as good as our bodies are at self-regulating, all systems eventually break down.

And yet, as Prigogine noted in his groundbreaking mid-twentieth-century research, many of the systems that make up our universe do *not* progress toward entropy. Evolution was, at the time Prigogine began publishing, a relatively new theory and a case in point. If systems tended toward entropy—if negative feedback loops balanced and rebalanced until the entire system broke down—then Prigogine questioned how completely new systems could ever come into being. How could we explain that some stimuli *did not* prompt a self-regulation, but, instead, caused the system to double down, leaning into the stimulus until something completely new was formed?

When he found the answer, they awarded him a Nobel prize.

His argument was deceptively simple, but it was also earth-shattering. While he didn't use the term, he essentially explained how catalysts—random, external stimuli —are the fabric of life itself. The concept goes well beyond the human experience, stretching across myriad scientific disciplines—as Prigogine argues, it explains the entire natural world as we know it.

That concept was the positive feedback loop.

If you've ever blown up a balloon, you've experienced a positive feedback loop. The balloon starts as a small, unimpressive item. Unlike its inflated siblings, an uninflated balloon is the farthest thing from festive.

But as soon as you begin to blow up the balloon—pushing air into the latex rubber shape—it begins to expand. As the warm air hits the latex, that too allows the balloon to expand even more. The effect keeps going. As the balloon grows larger and warmer, more air can fit inside. The more you blow, the faster the balloon expands.

This is an imperfect example of a positive feedback

loop, a series of reactions that move not toward self-regulation, but to increased chaos.

Of course, this example only works to a point. If you continue to blow up the balloon, the material will eventually reach its limit, and the exchange of energy will end. The system of molecules that make up the balloon will eventually give way, flinging energy carelessly around the space (and into your face if you're not careful).

That popped balloon becomes something new. Once the promise of a party, the balloon now represents something completely different—a piece of garbage that can never be returned to its original form.

This is the behavior of positive feedback loops in nature, and it was Prigogine's Nobel-prize-winning discovery, a complex theory whose essence explains the simplest, most fundamental properties of much of the known universe.

When a particular system meets a particular stimulus, Prigogine argues, that system may experience a critical transition—instead of self-regulating, the system instead feeds back into the stimulus, amplifying its effects. This happens over and over, until the system spins out of control. Then, something magical happens.

The entire system reorganizes into something new.

When I boarded that plane for Iceland, my relationship was self-regulating. Like all couples, we had disagreements from time to time, but they were always minor—things always resolved quickly and easily.

Our relationship was an open system, meaning it wasn't isolated from outside influences. It didn't exist in a vacuum. And it had evolved until it relied solely on the homeostasis of negative feedback loops. The relationship itself had become a self-regulating system with very little room for expansion or growth.

That Chapstick and the conversation it prompted was the external stimuli that turned the system on its head. A small prompt—me buying that Chapstick—triggered a conversation. That conversation was a catalyst—a small, unpredictable moment that had an outsized effect on my life—because my eventual response was not to self-regulate but to lean in to the opportunity I'd been presented.

An opportunity to evaluate, explore, and change.

I might have reacted with a regulatory response. Instead, I answered his question not with a reflexive "no," but with a curious "maybe."

Coco Chanel might have lost her business over the war. When fabric stores ran out of stock, she might have seen it as the natural breakdown of a system, a signal that the "arrow of time" had run its course for fashion, and that she should do something different.

Instead, she grabbed a bolt of jersey. She looked at the fashion industry—a system as old as time—and she saw a system spiraling toward entropy. Rather than reinventing the corset, she created something new.

And, suddenly, *POP*.

COCO CHANEL, CHAPSTICK, AND FEEDBACK LOOPS

Consider a single molecule simmering in a muddy, sludgy mass of molecules—a "primordial soup," as Ilya Prigogine and his co-author Isabelle Stengers called it. If we believe that the universe is ultimately driven by stability, as many have observed, then we might expect to see that bubbling, seething mass simply...continue to bubble and seethe.

But that's not what happened.

Instead, driven by some random, unknowable catalyst, a single molecule shifted.[4] It wasn't just any shift. It was the type of shift that prompts more of the same, one shift leading to another, and another, and another until that pile of primordial sludge took the shape of the original life in the universe.

It may or may not have happened spontaneously—with an outside stimulus sparking a change in a single, microscopic molecule. Either way, because the primordial soup responded with a positive feedback loop, life as we know it exists.

That outside stimulus was the original catalyst.

From the tiniest molecules to the entire universe, systems rule every aspect of our lives. Our cells balance and regenerate. Our bodies use those cells to sustain our respiratory, cardiovascular, and nervous systems. Those systems allow us to function in our family systems, and our family systems make up our social systems. Even our global ecosystems fit neatly within the solar system, which is undoubtedly part of even larger systems we have yet to discover.

Layer by layer, these systems use *negative* feedback loops to establish self-regulatory, predictable patterns.

That's a good thing in many instances.

Systems can be incredibly useful—you wouldn't be reading this without the combined forces of your body's systems, our system of language, and the educational system that taught you to read.

Systems are all around us.

But that's not the important part.

The important part is that not all systems march forward toward entropy. Sometimes, a regulatory response is replaced with a chain reaction. A tiny tube of Chapstick results in the birth of a child. A wartime fabric shortage results in the creation of today's most popular item of clothing.

If even one molecule of one aspect of any one of these systems were out of place, the moment you're experiencing right now might not have happened. Every moment in our lives—every experience, every thought, every bias, and even every surprise—all of them are systems. And those systems are made up of their own systems.

The "breeze" from a butterfly's wings isn't enough to start a tsunami, and in most cases, the "breeze" from the flipping of a page of a book won't change your life.

But in some cases, something as mundane as turning a page *can* change your life. You won't be able to predict it, precisely because it's baked into the cake of our lives, but those disturbances in the systems are part of the system, too, even though we don't typically think about things that way.

That's the thing about systems. They're only predictable because we've found a way to describe how they usually work. But with all systems, the tiniest disturbance can send them off-kilter.

And suddenly, everything can change.

PART TWO
TURBULENCE IS A FEATURE, NOT A BUG

CHAPTER 4
THE BOILING POINT

The average ten-year-old loses four baby teeth. The average ten-year-old is happy to do as their parents ask, although that behavior typically flips by the age of fifteen. The average ten-year-old enjoys socializing in groups and typically has a best friend of the same gender. The average ten-year-old is four-and-a-half feet tall.

By most measures, Sultan Kösen was an average ten-year-old. Growing up in the small village of Martin in southeastern Turkey, he enjoyed helping with chores around the house, particularly when it came to dusting things on high shelves or swiping the cobwebs off the ceiling. He enjoyed spending time with his friends, and most people in his small town knew him.

Mostly, he was average, but there was one exception.

At that age, Sultan was 6'6".

At some point during his short decade of life, a single cell near his temples sprouted into a clump. Each of the cells in that clump multiplied, and those cells multiplied, a positive feedback loop that created a tumor that pressed against his pituitary gland. Left unchecked, the tumor scrambled the signals that should have told Sultan's body to stop growing.

Eventually, his height made it impossible for him to attend school. At over eight feet tall, he was even too large to play basketball. Even things as simple as finding clothes that fit or moving through the narrow doorways of village homes proved challenging.

He spent his life severely depressed, resigned to a life of limitations. Around him, he saw people living average lives, doing all the things he couldn't do with an ease that felt extraordinarily unfair. Most of all, he longed for companionship. His dream in life was to start a family—to meet someone, fall in love, and marry them. Yet when he approached women, they often cowered in fear or literally ran away, frightened by his enormous height. All around him, his peers—the average people who had once been just like him—made lives for themselves.

All he could do was watch, depressed, lonely, and isolated, as his dreams seemed to become impossible.

Then, in 2009, he was officially recognized by the Guinness World Records as the tallest man in the world.

The recognition might have been seen as just a novelty for some, but Sultan saw it as his chance for a normal life. For the first time since that record-breaking growth spurt, he had access to the things he needed. He traveled the globe meeting world leaders, celebrities, and people from all walks of life, and the money he made from public appearances allowed him to pay for surgery to remove the tumor and stop his out-of-control growth.

He purchased clothing that was tailored to his stature, and began traveling with the Magic Circus of Samoa. And in 2013 he achieved the one thing he'd dreamed of since he was a boy.

He got married.

Prior to his recognition in the record book, women had been afraid of him. But with his newfound fame and fortune, he was able to meet the love of his life, a woman who, at 5'9", was herself taller than average.

Before the Guinness Book of World Records added him to their pages, he was hopeless. He rarely spoke, cowering from others in an attempt to make himself seem less frightening, more approachable.

After, he was a star.

It was as though someone had performed a magic trick on Sultan. As though with the flick of a magic wand, he went from lonely nobody to silly, outgoing, confident celebrity.

It was like he was a different person.

NOW, YOU SEE IT

A watched pot never boils, or at least that's what I learned growing up. Philosophically, the adage seems like simple advice—if we focus too much on the thing we want to happen, the time we have to wait can feel infinite.

Logistically, for the impatient among us, the phrase is also good advice. If you've ever watched a pot of water on the stove, perhaps waiting for the moment you can drop in your spaghetti or ramen, you'll recognize that the process builds up very slowly. First, a few tiny bubbles appear at the bottom of the pot. The color of the water almost seems to change, as air pockets cluster and clump far below the liquid's surface.

One or two of those bubbles eventually floats up to the surface of the water, followed by more. As the water grows hotter, the slow, steady march from one form to another, more bubbles rise to the top, perfectly spherical promises of the transition to come.

But even as those tiny pockets of air grow and multiply, they are still only promises. As long as the water remains below 212 degrees Fahrenheit—100 degrees Celsius—the water remains water. It can grow hotter and hotter, a straight line from its initial temperature carving a path toward its peak, but it cannot change states, no matter how long we wait and watch (or not watch, if you follow my grandmother's advice!).

It's not until the water molecules at the surface of the liquid gain enough energy to overcome the attractive forces holding them in the liquid phase that we can truly say the water is boiling. Those molecules suddenly—in an imperceptible instant—escape into the air as water vapor.

Whether you watch the pot or not, the water will boil, but even if you watch it very closely, your odds of catching the split second it reaches 212 degrees are low. One moment, it's a 211-degree liquid. The next, it's a 212-degree gas.

At first, the heat energy simply moves through water. Then, suddenly, the liquid radically restructures. As though the molecules have been trained and coached, they fall into a different formation—the tiniest marching band—spontaneously rearranging themselves into a brand-new shape with brand-new properties.

There's nothing less interesting than watching water boil, and maybe reading about it has the same somnambulant effect, so here's the point: the process of water boiling, where a liquid gets hotter and hotter until it reaches a tipping point and radically rearranges its molecules, is simply an example of a type of shift that has been observed in systems from physics to psychology.

Complex systems, as one team of psychology researchers led by Merlijn Olthof, of Radboud University Nijmegen, wrote, "have certain tipping points in which abrupt and discontinuous changes, called order transitions, from one system state to another occur."[1]

The shift from liquid to gas—from one state to another—is a common example of an order transition, a process also called a "phase transition" in fields like chemistry and thermodynamics.

What does the world's tallest man have in common with a pot of boiling water?

Both experienced an order transition.

At first glance, it may seem odd to use a moniker like *phase transitions* to describe a change in the trajectory of a life. But when Sultan describes how the Guinness Book of World Records changed his life, the near instantaneous shift is clear.

One day, he felt isolated and alone, unsure of how he would move forward in his life. That day, he had resigned himself to a life of difference, one that felt like a mark of social exclusion. He wasn't sure how he would go on. But he felt certain he would never reach a point of fulfillment in his life. He couldn't even attain his most basic goals—a steady, fulfilling job, a family of his own, or even the ability to walk down the street of a new place without passersby staring and pointing.

The next day was different. The next day, he was a record holder.

"After that day," Sultan explained to Ripley's, "I was born."

Of course, there was plenty of growth before Sultan reached the point of joining the Samoan Magic Circus.[2] He had to be the tallest ten-year-old before he could become the tallest man in his village, and he had to become the tallest man in his village before he could become the tallest man in the world.

But at 6'6", at 6'11", and even at seven and a half feet tall, he wasn't yet suitable for the Guinness Book of World Records. It wasn't until he reached 7'10"—the tipping point—that he transitioned from a very tall man to the tallest man in the world.

It wasn't Sultan's height alone that pushed him over the brink from his previous existence to his Guinness stardom. He'd been extremely tall for much of his life by that point, so crossing the threshold to tallest man alive was likely barely perceptible to the man and his community.

His life turned around when Guinness discovered him. The height was a prerequisite for this shift, but it wasn't the only component required for his transformation. The entire system needed to rearrange itself. So before he could reach the tipping point, the edges of these systems—of height, cultural context, and fame—blurred.

This is a key element of phase transitions. Near the

critical point—the tipping point at which a system that is organized one way transforms into a system that is organized in a different way—the lines between phases can appear blurred.

The bubbles begin to rise to the top, gaseous orbs within a liquid mass.

The bubbling, seething stew of pre-human goop begins to multiply in a very particular way, slowly (or at least potentially) taking on a new organizational system.

Or, in the lives of humans, the world rattles with promise, waiting for a single moment when change reaches critical mass.

And it's at this point, the aptly named "critical point," that a system grows even more connected with the systems around it.

The fashion industry vibrates against classic French music which buzzes with an assassin's bullet eight hundred miles away.

And yet, as complex as these systems appear to be—as complex as they *are*—changes like the one Coco Chanel experienced boil down to a single instant. One unexpected moment has an outsized impact on the trajectory of a life.

The same thing has happened to you, and the same thing happened to me. Sometimes, the tipping point is hard to miss—an incredible job offer or a winning lottery ticket. In other cases, the tipping point seems almost banal. A friend in college suggested I read Napoleon Hill's *Think and Grow Rich*, a book that had been published seventy years earlier. By the time I reached page 5, my perspective had already begun to shift—the water growing hotter and hotter—so that the ideas landed with an outsized force.

Reading that book was, for me, a moment everything changed.

The line graph of temperature and time looks steady. But when you wait for water to boil, you don't care much about what's happening at 211 degrees. You only care when you reach the critical point.

What makes these transitions so fascinating is not simply their ability to be cross-applied to a huge range of scientific disciplines—it's also the apparently magical way they work. On paper, these transitions seem gradual. But despite the gradual shift of particular elements *within* the system, the holistic shift of *the system itself* is not gradual at all.

The system shifts as quickly as the flip of a switch. As instantly as the snap of a finger. As startlingly sudden as a magician pulling a rabbit out of a hat.

Now, you see it.

Now, you don't.

But unlike the acts of the Samoan Magic Circus, the shift isn't a sleight of hand. When you watch water boil, you observe the radical transformation of one system to another. A stimulus—heat—prompts the initial slow-moving molecules of liquid to reorganize themselves into the rapidly moving molecules of gas. And while there is plenty of buildup in those dramatic moments—those moments when tiny bubbles cluster at the bottom of the pan and the molecules begin to vibrate in anticipation of their new arrangement—the transition itself is quick and decisive.

It only feels slow because we expect what's coming. We're watching the pot when we should be letting nature do its work.

A FORK IN THE ROAD

When we boil down Sultan's story to its before and after, the resulting narrative is undoubtedly oversimplified. The same is true for our example of boiling water—more happens in that unwatched pot than simply a rise in temperature and a shift in states.

Changes in air pressure can affect water's boiling point. An interruption in the heat source can short-circuit the rising temperature. Freezing external temperature can interfere with the boiling process. So could a hole in the pot.

And yet, when we think of a pot of boiling water, we're thinking of something that's relatively predictable.

Humans are not, in a word, predictable.

The concept of the tipping point—of order transitions —is only one piece of the puzzle. The other is related to the *type* of complex systems that behave the way water does, rising and shifting and seething and gurgling until —POP—the entire system spontaneously reorganizes itself.

This type of system is called a *dissipative structure.*

In simple terms, a dissipative structure is a type of complex system that constantly needs energy to function. In a way, a pot of boiling water fits this bill—if the heat energy ceases to flow, the water will remain water.

But when Prigogine began to study order transitions, he had a much more complex subject in mind: humans.

Since, as I discussed in the previous chapter, humans are open systems that constantly exchange energy and matter with our environment, we are, by definition, what we eat. And drink. And feel. And observe.

Every single bit of energy we take in is part of and the result of its own system, which makes things very difficult to predict—there are *a lot* of variables to account for when we start to think about all of our connections with the outside world.

Prigogine called complex systems like these dissipative structures, which simply means systems that draw energy from outside of themselves to survive.

But the terminology he used might be the least interesting part of his theory. Because what Prigogine discovered was that dissipative structures—from individual humans to weather systems to entire societies—very often come to a point that forces a decision.

These forks in the road follow periods of turbulence and instability, like our pot of boiling water, except in dissipative systems the tipping point isn't so predictable. In dissipative systems, things can go any number of ways.

They can change states, flipping to a qualitatively different state of being in the blink of an eye.

Or they can stay exactly as they are, pushing through the increased energy, pressure, and tension to maintain the same basic make-up, for better or for worse.

Sultan could have continued to do the best he could with what he had. For the rest of his life, his body might have continued to grow larger and larger, his organs crowding each other and his joints straining under the pressure of his weight, until he eventually died. He could have lived a lifetime without clothing that fit, without a life partner, without a career he loved.

But a random event struck—the Guinness Book of World Records certified his height and listed him in their volume. He couldn't control what the Guinness people did, and he couldn't really have known what would come from the listing. But rather than shrinking away from a new arrangement, he leaned in to the change. He allowed the outside energy of the record book to flip his world on its head.

"PRETTY GOOD...BUT NOT GREAT"

It's perhaps unexpected that a former US secretary of state shares a name with a musical notation. But Condoleezza Rice's name was taken from an Italian notation—*con* meaning "with," and *dolcezza*, "sweetness." Her mother was a teacher and church organist who loved opera, particularly Italian opera, so she gifted her daughter with a name pulled from the most treasured scores of Puccini and Monteverdi.

Perhaps she dreamed that her daughter would become a musician—maybe a pianist and organist like her mother. Maybe an opera singer on the world's stages.

It was a tall order for the great grandchild of an enslaved woman.

In the time between her great grandmother gaining such favor with her enslaver that he taught her to read—nearly unheard of in the antebellum South—and when

Condoleezza was born, much had changed. And much had remained the same.

Black children were allowed to attend schools, albeit segregated ones.

But even today, fewer than 2 percent of classical musicians are Black. In the late 1950s the landscape was even bleaker for an African American concert pianist.

In spite of how steeply the odds were stacked against her, Condoleezza excelled in school and music. She attended Birmingham's segregated schools beginning in second grade. She was too advanced to start in first grade with other students her age.

But no amount of brightness could protect a young Black girl growing up in 1960s Birmingham. On Sunday morning September 15, 1963, eight-year-old Condoleezza was at her father's church when she felt a blast—a sound that would reverberate through her ears for the rest of her life. Just a few blocks away, a bomb had gone off at 16th Street Baptist Church, killing four little girls about her age.

One of them was Condoleezza's friend and playmate, Denise McNair.

As Condoleezza would later recall, "the crime was calculated to suck the hope out of young lives, bury their aspirations. But those fears were not propelled forward, those terrorists failed."

Instead, the event etched a mantra in her mind—it would take determination to rise to the challenge of adversity. As the African American proverb goes, she would have to be twice as good to get half as much as her white peers.

The situation was unfair, but Condoleezza was up to the task. Not only did she soar through her schooling, skipping not only the first grade but also later the seventh, she also excelled at music. Trained on the piano from a very young age, the little girl was something of a prodigy.

She majored in music and, as a college sophomore who was only seventeen years old, she attended the Aspen Music Festival and School, one of the most prestigious training events in the country, particularly for young adults. The highly selective event still runs—by application only—and currently attracts up to 100,000 audience members who come to watch college and graduate students perform.

By all accounts, her star was rising, the momentum of her burgeoning performance career beginning to bubble with promise. She was climbing rapidly toward the pinnacle of success for concert pianists.

So were dozens of other performers.

During the two-month run of the Aspen Music Festival and School, participants can choose from four hundred events, including concerts and master classes.

Condoleezza drank in the music. She was moved by the heart she heard in the music of other pianists—the way they infused their music with something that was much greater than the sum of its parts. As she listened, she *felt* as much as heard the performers. There was a message. A connection. A community.

When these performers played, they did more than simply hit the right notes in the written sequence. They brought the music to life.

And they were twelve years old.

That moment made her realize something. She could never play like that. Even though she was only seventeen at the time, she felt light years behind these young prodigies in terms of her skill.

As she later told the Kunhardt Film Foundation, she realized she was "pretty good at this but not great."

At this point, some might have stepped in to comfort her. "No, no, don't give up," I can imagine them saying. "You'll get there! Just keep working!"

But I'm not sure the young prodigy needed comfort.

The story could be framed as one of disappointment and broken dreams. After all, Condoleezza could not have predicted or controlled the moment she sat in that darkened concert hall and realized she would never become a truly great concert pianist. The moment happened *to* her, a twist of fate that spoiled a two-decade-old dream.

But catalysts are about much more than disappointment. In fact, it's worth clarifying that catalysts aren't about making the most of a bad situation, although they can appear that way from the outside.

What catalysts are really about is the moment everything changes—the moment you reach a tipping point, a point at which remaining where you are is the equivalent of turning off the heat.

Choosing to stay water, despite being on the brink of transforming into steam.

For so many people whose lives have been changed by catalysts, that moment wasn't about disappointment. It was about crossing a threshold.

After Condoleezza's fateful concert moment, she wasn't sure what to do next.

But she was smart and curious—and determined—so she went home and told her parents she was changing her major. To what, she wasn't sure.

Months later, she stumbled into Josef Korbel's International Politics course. Korbel was a world-renowned expert on Russian politics (not to mention Madeline Albright's father!), and his teaching opened up a new world for Condoleezza, one that she'd never considered before.

And it fascinated her.

"All of a sudden," she later recalled, "I knew what I wanted to do."[3]

That moment of clarity was more decisive than anything she'd felt with her music.[4] It was a burst of energy that told her exactly what to do, where to go, and why.

TURN THE PAGE

Two years after the four little girls were murdered by a bomb in their church, the citizens of Watts, Los Angeles, rose up. After years of police brutality, economic inequality, and social injustice, the neighborhood's mostly Black citizens launched a wake-up call to the nation, demanding attention to the urgent need for racial equality and justice.

That moment was sparked by rumors that a Black motorist—Marquette Frye—had been brutally beaten while being arrested by the California highway patrol.

Twenty-five years later, another motorist would be beaten by California police, and the citizens of Los Angeles would once against rise up against the violence they'd seen since long before Frye's arrest. The video of Rodney King being beaten by four police officers was perhaps the world's first viral video, and it set off a shock wave that was felt across the country, a rush of righteous anger that mimicked what had happened generations before.

Violence and oppression had been directed at LA's Black community for decades. Frye wasn't the first motorist to be beaten, and King wasn't the second.

The two men were part of a long, brutal legacy. The news of their beatings were flashpoints in history—points at which the water could no longer bear to remain water.

Those beatings were tipping points.

As a child recently taken from his family and placed in a foster home in Los Angeles, Na'im Al-Amin felt them deeply.

When eight-year-old Na'im arrived in the 1980s—having been removed from Junction City, Kansas, a town with a population under twenty thousand people—he had never seen graffiti. He didn't understand what gangs were. He'd never seen a dead body. And he had certainly never been arrested.

By his tenth birthday, all of that had changed.

He was arrested at eight years old, an experience he describes as "formatively terrifying." At that point, he knew in his blood that he was marginalized—that he had been, as the phrase Ibram X. Kendi later popularized, "stamped from the beginning."

But it was what happened a year later that etched in his mind. With the wiry headphones of the 1980s clamped over his ears and a West Coast rap compilation carrying him through the day, he walked out of a friend's house to witness a man's murder.

Police arrived to cover the body, except, as is often the case in Black neighborhoods, officers chose to leave the body partially exposed.

The image of a white sheet with a brown arm sticking out, of the red blood left to turn tarry and black on the pavement, burned itself into Na'im's mind.

"I'm going to die soon," the nine-year-old thought. To hear him tell the story now, you can hear the resolution in the phrase. In a single moment of clarity, he simply *knew* that his life was about to end.

The rest of his time in Los Angeles followed this trajectory, one that was very different from the life he might have lived with his nuclear family.

As he grew into a teenager, his experiences of violence, oppression, and disregard climbed steadily, his environment growing hotter and hotter with each passing day.

And then, one of his best friends was murdered.

Now legally an adult, he fled back to the Midwest, where he would attend college with me at Kansas State University. When I met Na'im, he described his time in Los Angeles as a "ten-year tour of duty." A war zone.

Just as that murderous bomb resonated in Condoleezza's ears for decades after the fact, the trauma of being surrounded by gun violence—as a child, alone, over a thousand miles from your family—has a way of lingering.

All of those sounds had changed Na'im like Condoleezza before him, but he was resilient, and he set out to change his own life. The change wouldn't be instantaneous or even unpredictable—this time, he had to introduce a stimulus to his own life. But he hoped it would lay the groundwork for something better, even if he couldn't imagine what it was.

And, truly, it would have been impossible to predict what eventually changed his life.

During Na'im's time at K-State, he and I got to know each other through the Student Government Association. One afternoon, in a chance conversation, I gave him *Think and Grow Rich*. It was a book I'd read shortly before, a book that had been published seventy years prior, but a book that I felt still carried a good deal of resonance. It had inspired me to take control of my own destiny.

We'd had some conversation that made me think of that book, and I knew he'd love it, so I handed it off to him —an inexpensive gift, but one that I knew could change his life. It had changed mine.

I don't remember whether we talked much about the book, or if I even followed up to see if he'd read it at the time. We both had busy lives.

When our time at K-State drew to an end, we both graduated, full of optimism about our futures and brimming with visions of the amazing things we would do next. We fell out of touch, as is so often the case following a graduation, until one day I went to my bookshelf to grab a paperback. Next to the book I needed was Napoleon Hill's *Think and Grow Rich*.

Instantly, I thought of Na'im.

I Googled him, and when the result came up, I gasped. He was serving time in prison on a conspiracy drug charge. He'd refused to testify against a friend, and now his entire future was in jeopardy.

In a way, it was difficult to reconcile the idea that Na'im was in jail—I'd known him as an ambitious, driven guy who planned to go to law school after college.

In another, it made sense. Na'im had always been fiercely loyal, a dedicated friend who showed so much passion for helping others. It made sense that he would refuse to turn on a friend.

Still, it was hard to think about him being swallowed up by the system—of being sucked in and beat up the way Marquette Frye had been. The way Rodney King had been.

So I scrawled a quick message on a postcard. "*Think and Grow Rich*," I wrote, recalling the book that had changed my life. The book that I knew could change his. "I still believe in you."

I didn't think much of it after that point. While I thought about Na'im from time to time, we'd gone our separate ways, and our relationship became more of a fond memory than an active part of my life.

Later, when Na'im and I caught up, he told me that my postcard had changed his life. "It elevated my self-efficacy to a point that I could believe in myself," he said.

We hadn't talked for four years before that.

When he read the postcard, he told me, he remembered the concept of ideation, Napoleon Hill's idea that we can take control of our lives by visualizing the outcomes we want to achieve—and by believing in them without wavering. And he remembered Hill's advice to reach out to those who can help you along your journey.

He'd seen so much during his time in prison. He'd seen the same kinds of abuse and violence he'd experienced during his time in LA, but more than that, he'd seen how difficult it was to build a life after incarceration. During his time in prison, he saw people return who had been released. He saw the hopelessness and the sense that there was nothing better waiting on the outside.

He remembered how he'd been stamped from the beginning—that first arrest at eight years old—and he knew he had to take control. He had to help others find their value and build their lives the way he had been able to do after he received that postcard.

The ideas had bubbled in him since he was a child, growing up Black in a white foster family, witnessing death from such a young age, being treated as though he was already part of the prison system years before he was old enough to drive a car.

But one piece was missing. When I dropped that postcard in the mail, I had no idea that it would push him to the tipping point—that it would be the last degree on the thermometer before Na'im's life transformed. From water to steam. From graphite to a diamond. From prisoner to entrepreneur.

He still had one year to serve, but he'd reached a critical point. During his last year in prison, he wrote a business plan for a nonprofit organization that would be called "Swagg, Inc," a company name that stands for "Serve Witness And Give Guidance, Inspiration Never Ceases." The organization would help previously incarcerated people build new lives for themselves through education, employment training, and entrepreneurship.

From an outside perspective, Na'im might have appeared the same. He was still incarcerated. He continued to read voraciously. He occupied the same cell he had the day before.

But in his mind, he'd reached 212 degrees, and his entire outlook—his entire identity—shifted in an instant.

He was still a prisoner. Now, he felt free.

A STIMULUS AND A TRANSFORMATION

That feeling of transformative freedom looks different for everyone. Some people are radically transformed while reading an amazing book. Others experience critical points during thoughtful, intimate conversations.

In many cases, the first recognizable tipping point we experience occurs within an educational context. As Condoleezza later described of her own teaching experiences, "In a class of twenty, there are always two or three for whom the lights go on."

The metaphor is apt: one moment things look murky. The next, the world appears in technicolor. We take in so much information every single day. And suddenly, along comes a single, electric idea—one anecdote, one example, one piece of data—that tips us over the brink.

Think and Grow Rich changed me. Profoundly. And, although I had no idea whether or how it would work, when I dropped that postcard in the mail, I hoped it might be the stimulus Na'im needed to change his life, too.

Every person I've mentioned in this book—every person in the world, I would venture to guess—has experienced something similar. Out of nowhere, an unexpected flash of heat strikes, and we're never the same.

The entire process is completely unpredictable, and often, it's difficult to believe how something so tiny could transform us so instantly and so fully.

There's a simple explanation for this.

When we look back at our lives before the tipping point, we're looking back on someone completely different. We're steam rising from the pot looking back at our lukewarm past selves. Sometimes it's difficult to make sense of how we survived back then. Sometimes people even describe that time as a "past life," a phrase that's often meant to lighten the mood after a major career or life transition, but a phrase that's packed with meaning.

When we experience a catalyst, from landing an agent to buying a tube of Chapstick to running into an old acquaintance, the effects can be profound. Like the tallest man in the world, they are, by definition, outsized.

And yet, this process happens every single day—constantly—in our world. Water boils. Chemicals transform. People read books.

As Prigogine argued in his Nobel prize–winning research, "Only when a system behaves in a sufficiently random way may the difference between past and future, and therefore irreversibility, enter into its description...The arrow of time is the manifestation of the fact that the future is not given."

Prigogine proved that the universe's ability to transform—randomly—was the very basis for life itself. The right combination of heat, light, and pressure clicked into place and a muddy bog transformed into a Petri dish for the first sparks of life on earth.

The idea seems so profound that it's difficult to fully comprehend.

Until you realize that this type of change happens every day.

A very tall man becomes a celebrity.

A little girl from Birmingham becomes the secretary of state.

A prisoner becomes an entrepreneur.

And all it takes is a single second.

CHAPTER 5
SOME MINOR TURBULENCE

When you travel by plane, your body moves through space at a rate of around six hundred miles per hour—about eight times faster than the speed limit on most interstate highways. Factors like controlled cabin pressure and the constancy of speed mean that we don't usually think about that speed—apart from the brief period of take-off and landing—just like we don't feel our bodies moving through space when we travel by car or train.

Unless something goes wrong.

Think about the last time your flight hit "rough air." You might have felt a sudden drop, and your stomach probably lurched, as though it had jumped into your throat. The *ding ding ding* of the "fasten seatbelts" sign added to the rush of adrenaline, as did the flight attendants moving quickly to the front and back of the cabin to fasten their seatbelts. You felt yourself jostled through the air, heard a baby scream, and saw the look of fear on at least one of your fellow travelers.

The jolt to the senses is a sudden, visceral reminder that you are moving very quickly through the air, six or seven miles above the ground. Walking, it takes the average person about two hours to travel seven miles. Falling takes considerably less time.

When your plane hits significant turbulence, you suddenly become viscerally, sickeningly aware of how far you have traveled and how much farther you have to go.

You might pray to be back where you started—to never have left in the first place.

You might wonder at human folly, to think such a technology could ever truly be safe.[1]

You might hope for a runway below you. It wouldn't be the worst thing in the world to enjoy a short layover in Denver, right? You've always loved spending time in the mountains, after all!

Those moments of instability—of feeling like you're in a tin can that's being violently shaken by an excited toddler—can be overwhelming.

But if you travel often, you've likely come to realize that turbulence is simply a part of flying. The longer the voyage, the more likely that parts of the flight will be unpleasant.

You probably also realize that those patches of rough air are just that—patches. If you can breathe deeply and ignore the person retching two rows behind you, you'll be fine in a few minutes. And, anyway, there's no other choice. There's no way out but through.

POP THE CORK

One evening in September 1944, Alistair Urquhart was moving very quickly through space. But he wasn't flying through the air—he was being propelled through the water. Suddenly and without warning, Alistair had been ejected from the open hatch of the *Kachidoki Maru* as it sank violently to the bottom of the South China Sea. "I popped out of the ship," he later wrote, "like a cork out of a champagne bottle."[2]

The water felt cold, and he choked on the oil that spewed from the sinking vessel and eleven others around it. The sea was known for being infested with sharks, and he had no supplies, no life preserver, and no sense of where the nearest land might be.

It was, perhaps, the best thing that had happened to him in five years.

When World War II broke out, Alistair had been conscripted into the British Army. He was assigned to a troop known as the Gordon Highlanders, and by the end of 1941, he found himself sweating through his wool uniform as his company fought to hold the line against Japan's siege of Singapore.

The ineptitude of those British forces has been well-documented, both by historians and by Alistair himself, who recalls being forced to take a daily nap while Japanese forces continued to gain ground in the skirmish.

Perhaps as a result of poor planning on the part of the English Army, or perhaps by random chance, Alistair and his colleagues were captured. In February 1942 he was one of tens of thousands of Allied troops who were forced to march to the Japanese prison camps. The walk was grueling, and not only physically. By design, their somber route led them past unspeakable horrors. Alistair later recalled the terror of seeing mass graves—perhaps intended for him and his fellow marchers—and rows of decapitated heads suspended on spikes.

The spectacle was a brutally effective form of psychological warfare that aimed to destabilize the nervous system and decrease resistance. It was intended to convey a sense of helplessness to the prisoners.

And that's precisely what Alistair was—a prisoner.

In his memoir, he describes the moment he realized that his identity had changed. As his colleagues trudged forward, the idea struck him like a fist to the jaw. "It was a gut-wrenching realization to think that my liberty was gone and no telling for how long it would be so," he wrote in his autobiography. "This was the worst moment of my life."

Yanked from the life he'd always known, and with little warning or preparation, his entire system had been thrown on its axis.

He had been a young man of only twenty before he left home to fight.

Now, he was a prisoner.

As the days turned to weeks and weeks turned to years, the shocking terror of that initial realization gave way to true horror. Shipped into the Thailand jungle in cramped, putrid train cars, the prisoners would be forced to build the Burma Railroad. That railroad would later earn the moniker "Death Railroad," because "one man died for every [rail tie] laid."[3]

By the time Alistair was taken aboard the submarine in early 1944, he'd seen hundreds of men die. He'd lived more than a week in solitary confinement (a punishment for resisting the sexual advances of a prison guard). And he'd eaten nothing but watery, vermin-infested rice for 750 days.

He thought things couldn't get any worse.

That was when he was forced to board the *Kachidoki Maru*.

Packed into the tight, airless ship's hold, he and countless other prisoners were left to rot. The dark space wouldn't even allow them to count the days, and by all accounts, the time stretched on endlessly. "I never thought anything could ever match the terror of the railway," Alistair said. "Being in the hold was worse. At least while slaving on the railway you could move. And you had fresh air."[4]

The sounds of the hold must have been more gruesome than any 1980s slasher film.

But soon, an even more ominous sound would flood the background. That sound signaled imminent death. A present attack. It was the sound of a US submarine torpedoing the steamship.

And then, Alistair was flying.

CHANGE IS NOT LINEAR

How could someone like Alistair ever return to life as a civilian? How could he recover some semblance of hope? Could he ever be the same?

Clinical psychology researchers have spent decades

searching for data-based approaches to healing trauma. And in many cases, science has created new pathways for traveling from surviving to thriving. The research itself is far from easy, but most projects follow a simple, tried-and-true experimental design formula:

1. Participants are recruited for the study.
2. Participants complete a baseline assessment.
3. Participants experience some kind of an intervention—typically a training, a treatment, or a series of exercises.
4. Participants take a post-test to assess their psychological state after the intervention.
5. Participant data is aggregated, cleaned, and analyzed, and the average pre-test score is compared with the average post-test score to determine whether the intervention has effectively changed the subject's state.

In practice, things are more complicated than simple averages. Psychology researchers use many advanced statistical tools to ensure that their data is as sound as possible. Data analysis is rarely as simple as averaging two sets of numbers—typically there is a complex procedure for adjusting the data to account for anticipated deviations. Researchers check the results to ensure that they are statistically significant (i.e., stronger than we would expect from random chance). And the data is cleaned for noise: seemingly random, individual deviations that stray far enough from the average are to be considered outliers.

This practice—of dismissing individual participants'

data from research studies when it deviates from a group average—was the subject of a groundbreaking meta-analysis published by a University of Delaware research team.

Their argument was simple. If you remove all of the outliers from a dataset, then compare the average scores for pre-test and post-test, you'll end up with something that looks very tidy—two dots on a simple line graph.

Draw a line between them, and you communicate a very clear—but very inaccurate—idea: change is linear.

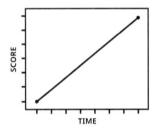

Figure 5.1. Average change for a study population between pre- and post-tests

The problem is that complex systems never transform in such a neat and predictable manner. And, as I have discussed throughout this book, as complex systems that contain and operate within other complex systems, human brains don't either.

The Delaware-based team, led by Dr. Adele M. Hayes, knew that psychological change was almost never linear. As they'd seen in their own research—and their own lives—most of us don't move in a single straight line from sick to healthy. We struggle through periods of instability, false wins, failure, elation, and despair on our paths to eventual growth.

In substance abuse cases, for instance, Hayes and her team identified a common trend: patients would experience profound instability, their overall mental health scores bouncing up and down from week to week or even day to day. Some short periods would appear stable. Those would often be followed by a frantic rise and fall, rise and fall, rise and fall—like the blips on a heart monitor.

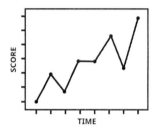

Figure 5.2. Real change for an average study participant as measured at multiple points between pre- and post-tests

Dr. Hayes had seen how a profoundly *unstable* period could suddenly resolve itself, concluding with a clear, definitive improvement.

It wasn't just that patients needed to go through the period of turbulence to come out of the experience stronger. That kind of conclusion is great for self-help books and Hallmark movies.

The point was that the period of turbulence actually *predicted* patients' immediate outcomes—as Hayes and her team pointed out, observing daily mental health metrics could tell psychologists when a patient was about to have a breakthrough.

The frantic rise and fall on the line graph of progress isn't "noise." It's evidence that the system has been knocked on its axis, that the subject has been introduced to a new stimulus of some kind. And that stimulus has thrown the whole system—as well as every connected system—completely out of whack.

Hayes argued that if clinicians recognized that periods of instability don't necessarily signal an impending failure —they just as often signal impending progress—they could adjust their approaches with patients. They could embrace the turbulence with the understanding that rough air is just part of the journey.

If you think about your own experiences of major life change, I'll bet you've seen this happen. You experienced a catalyst that profoundly rattled you. Maybe you stumbled upon a job opportunity too good to pass up, one that required moving across the country to a city you'd never visited. Maybe a friend's offhand remark made you realize you'd outgrown your personal network, which made you realize you needed a new social circle, a new place to hang out, or entirely new habits. Maybe you saw an ad on Facebook for an interesting certification program that led your life in an entirely new direction.

Whatever your catalyst, I'll bet some time passed between experiencing that catalyst and experiencing the life that came as a result.

You were thrilled for the new job opportunity, but had to rediscover the simplest things—where to shop for groceries, who to see for dentist appointments, where to meet new friends.

Or you let go of the relationship, but still found yourself reaching for the phone to text your new ex from time to time. Sometimes, you felt a little lonely. You had to say goodbye to some inside jokes and get used to being on your own.

Or you set out to write a business plan...even though you didn't know much about business. Suddenly, writing a business plan wasn't just writing a business plan—it was reading unfamiliar books, trying (and erroring) to make sense of financial projects, and trashing *a lot* of early efforts before you finally landed on an idea that worked.

And yet, due to the nature of phase transitions, you *were* changed. Even before you landed on that new sense of stability—the new job, the new relationship, the new life plan—you knew there was no going back.

So you struggled through the rocky times, pushing forward every single day, until suddenly things felt different. Finally the systems of your everyday life caught up to your newly transformed identity.

That's the type of experience Dr. Hayes and her team wanted to document—they wanted to explore not just the end result of change but the rough air we all pass through before we reach our eventual our destination, whatever that might be.

STEPPING INTO THE MATRIX

In 2010 an image raced across cyberspace, spreading rapidly from niche message boards to mainstream social media to our collective imagination. In the picture, a man slumps on a bench. He wears jeans and a simple blazer, and his elbows are propped on his knees, his gaze pointing downwards toward the pavement. With a half-eaten sandwich drooping from his hand, his soberly contemplative expression looks almost like a caricature of pain. It's as if, lost in morose thoughts, the man has forgotten he was eating a sandwich, forgotten he was in public, forgotten his purpose entirely.

Given the man's familiar face, the image prompted not only meme-worthy captions but also concerned speculations. The man's posture spoke not of a Hollywood icon but of a depleted soul, overwhelmed with unbearable emotional weight.

We thought we'd seen every side of this man. We'd seen his tender side in *The Lakehouse* four years earlier. The year prior, he'd played the titular character in the paranormal thriller *Constantine*. And we'd seen him contemplate red pills and blue pills a decade before.

We'd known him since he was just a teenager, traveling through time in a totally excellent phone booth.

How could Keanu Reeves—a man who had earned over $40 million for a single movie franchise—be so exaggeratedly sad?

What most commenters likely didn't realize was that Keanu had more to mourn than any one person should. The actor's life had been pockmarked by tragedy and loss, although he remained relatively quiet about them.

When the actor was just three years old, his father left their family. Keanu was barely a teenager the last time he saw his father.

In 1992 Keanu's sister Kim was diagnosed with leukemia, and the actor took time away from his rapidly growing film career to spend time with his ailing sister.

The year after Kim's diagnosis, Keanu's best friend—River Phoenix—died of a drug overdose.

It seemed as though the young actor's career was catapulting him to success while his personal life plummeted into despair. But despite the instability that threatened to swallow him whole, he pressed on through what he must have thought would be the most challenging period of his life.

And then, just a year before *The Matrix* carved Keanu's name into Hollywood history, the actor began dating actress and production assistant Jennifer Syme.

The relationship was life-changing for both of them as, by all accounts, they fell instantly, madly in love. Within a year, Jennifer was pregnant, and the two looked forward to raising a family together. As Christmas of 1999 approached, Jennifer went into labor. The eager couple rushed to the hospital to welcome Ava Archer Syme-Reeves into the world.

But the little girl would never take her first breath.

Flung once more into heart-wrenching instability, Keanu now struggled not only with the loss of his daughter—but also with his partner's soul-crushing grief.

As though the actor had not been given enough to handle, Jennifer died less than two years later. She was driving home from a party and lost control of her vehicle, crashing into a row of parked cars. She was thrown from the car and died instantly.

Life had dealt Keanu one blow after another, barely giving him time to breathe between tragedies.

It's difficult—and unnecessary—to find a "silver lining" in a series of senseless fatalities. These experiences of loss are heart-breaking, and they deserve to be acknowledged and accepted as such.

There is no happy ending when it comes to losing one person after another to senseless, inexplicable tragedy.

But even without a happy ending—even with no ending in sight at all—survivors are left to pick up the pieces.

In an interview with *Parade* in 2006, Keanu spoke about his grief, reflecting on the impact it had on his life. "Grief changes shape," he shared, "but it never ends... Much of my appreciation of life has come through loss. Life is precious. It's worthwhile."[5]

When his life began to move up and down like the blips of a heart monitor, Keanu could have settled into a bitter, disillusioned perspective. He could have grown numb from the pain.

Or he could look at things in a different way, allowing his experiences of loss to drive him to embrace life. He could leverage his horrible, intimate understanding of the value of life by paying forward all of his *good* fortune.

All of these are new routes to stability. All can be the result of destabilizing events.

And all are just as valid as every other.

But all results that involve a total and permanent shift —a phase transition—require us to pass through a period of instability. There's simply no other way to achieve lasting, noticeable change.

SINGIN' IN THE RAIN

By the time Alistair was ejected from the *Kachidoki Maru*, his life had already been irreparably destabilized. He had undergone an absolute transformation, one that left him emaciated, bald, and on the constant brink of death.

He later spoke about his will to live, remarking with fascination that the younger men—those who had been just teenagers when they were taken prisoner by the Japanese—should have been the most resilient in their jungle death march. Instead, it was the thirty- and forty-something men who had the highest survival rate.

Alistair attributed this fact to their will to live. For his older peers, having something to return to was motivation to survive each day. And while Alistair's life looked somewhat different from his peers with wives and children waiting back home, he found their tenacity inspiring.

That's why, when he was spit out of the submarine like chewed-up kelp, he swam hard away from the sinking ship.[6] He clung to a single-person life raft through the long, terrible night. As he floated there in shark-infested waters, he listened as the prisoners he'd worked beside just days earlier groaned and screamed. Finally, the night went quiet, although it's difficult to say whether the silence was a result of Alistair floating out of earshot or another, horrifying cause.

It would be four days before he was recaptured by a Japanese whaler and dropped at a port on Hainan Island where other shipwrecked POW survivors waited. The survivors, who had all come so close to death—sunburned, dehydrated, and emaciated—were forced to walk through the village to the camp naked in the pouring rain.

And then came a note of revelry.

"I'm siiiiiingin' in the rain," one man crooned.

Others joined in, forming an unlikely chorus of the tormented. Soon, they were reworking the lyrics to deride and mock their captors.[7]

From Hainan, Alistair was sent to another prison camp, a few miles outside of Nagasaki, where he would be reunited with one of the most inspiring figures he'd met in the jungle: Dr. Mathieson. A family physician before his capture, Dr. Mathieson had saved countless men on Death Railroad, offering innovative remedies that used what little supplies he had available as well as very effective placebo treatments.

Dr. Mathieson had saved Alistair's life, in fact, helping him to cure a potentially deadly infection with a medieval-sounding treatment that's not for the faint of heart.[8]

Encountering the doctor again inspired Alistair, who had already survived more than any one person could be expected to. Now, Alistair studied beside Dr. Mathieson, taking in his knowledge of medicine as well as his kindness, patience, and care.

Alistair's life had been turned upside down. From his original capture to the horrors of the jungle to being ejected from a sinking ship, he had been without stability for some time. But since the moment he transformed—the moment he realized that he was a prisoner—he had never stopped learning.

After that final capture, Alistair lay on the floor of his

hut one night and made a "silent vow to spend the rest of [his] life bettering the lot of others."[9]

When he transformed from soldier to prisoner, the transformation had been bleak. It was the type of catalyst that's nearly impossible to miss.

But subtle as it was, the conversation Alistair had with Dr. Mathieson—the one that inspired him to serve others —was a catalyst, too. The turbulence had not broken, but that conversation had given him a way to ride it out—to build a home in the instability and do what he could to find peace amid the hell he'd been plunged into.

On August 9, 1945, the still-young man was tending a vegetable garden for the Japanese officers of the camp when he heard a clap of thunder. The sound stopped him in his tracks, and he rested his hoe on the ground and turned toward the origin of the noise, somewhere in the city.

A few moments later, he felt a blast of heat, the outermost effects of the atomic bomb that destroyed Nagasaki. The force knocked him off his feet.

And it saved his life.

That bomb marked the beginning of the end, a catalyst that truly signaled his departure from one phase to another—not from soldier to prisoner, but from prisoner to civilian.

From captivity to freedom.

When Alistair pens his autobiography at the age of ninety, the first word he uses to describe himself is "lucky." He rejoices in having survived the worst possible circumstances and being blessed with living a long life, noting, "I have not allowed my life to be blighted by bitterness. At ninety years of age I have lived a long life and continue to live it to the fullest."[10]

Alistair lived a life of turbulence that most of us couldn't even imagine, repeatedly falling the equivalent of seven miles to earth. He faced the extremes of disease, cruelty, and deprivation, experiences that scarred him for life. His stomach had shrunk such that he could only ever eat carefully in small, easy amounts for the rest of his life. Oil that he swallowed while escaping the sinking ship damaged his vocal cords. Cancers appeared later in his life that he linked with prolonged exposure to the sun during his time on the Death Railroad.

He also carried with him the memories of the small bright moments in the dark. Working alongside Dr. Mathieson taught him the deep value of helping others even when you have little. Singing naked in the rain with his fellow defiant, unbroken prisoners gave him a renewed pride.

Until his death in 2016, just three years shy of a century of life, Alistair was an avid ballroom dancer. He took up the hobby after the war and incorporated it into his everyday life, a small, joyful expression—a revelry of freedom and ease.

Through the turbulence, and even after, he'd changed many times. With each change came instability. And sometimes, that instability predicted something profound.

Systems shift. Alistair knew that better than most. By leaning into the tilted axis of his life—embracing the turbulence—he matched his trauma with service, advocacy, and hope, messages that survive long after his death through his harrowing autobiography.

TRAVEL GUIDES

Just a year after the meme-able image of Keanu spread across the web like wildfire, the actor penned a tongue-in-cheek poetry collection which he called *Ode to Happiness*. The poems, which started as an inside joke between friends, are comically morose.

"I draw my hot sorrow bath," one reads. "Wash my face with regret shampoo."

As if to drive home the book's depressive sentiments—and point out the absurdity of these periods in our lives—the lines are accompanied by grayscale illustration. The "grown-up's picture book" emphasizes the sardonic humor that has provided a lifeline for Keanu through layers and layers of instability.[11]

And yet, while many might define his life as tormented or, movie stardom aside, despairing, Keanu has dedicated his life to helping others. The things that transformed him—losing a baby, a partner, a best friend—changed who he was. That's true, whether you look for a silver lining or not.

Based on Dr. Hayes's research and the actor's own words, it seems possible that his profound transformation was not just a byproduct of trauma. Rather, the instability that he experienced as a result of losing everything became a predictor for something larger to come.

It's not magic.

And while it *is* science, it isn't complicated. When we're shaken to our cores, we *must* find our centers. We have no choice but to stabilize. One option is to backpedal —we can scramble to regain our former stability. Another is to embrace the finality of death, moving through self-destructive behaviors toward the ultimate stability.

Or we can take a third route. We can lean into the opportunity for a new world, redefining who we are, what we do, and how much we are capable of.

A few years after the candid park photo became the "sad Keanu" meme, the actor chuckled about it with Stephen Colbert. In his interview on *The Late Show*, he laughed, "I was hungry."

It seems few Hollywood celebrities can have long careers without earning a few scars on their reputations, but Keanu has become known as one of the nicest guys in in the industry. Stories abound of generous gifts to the hardworking gaffers and kind interactions with fans. His career has continued on a steady upward trajectory for nearly forty years, from his first television series in 1984 to today where, in addition to being the leading man in several continuing franchises, he also lends his voice to video games and animated movies and performs with his alternative rock band Dogstar.

He knows well that grief lives on. He also seems to understand the worst moments—the moments where the ground falls from beneath you and suddenly you're in freefall—don't last forever. Eventually, the path levels out again, and if you step back far enough, you can see that the path, despite all the pits and sudden falls, goes steadily up.

WHEN THE SYSTEMS TILTS

The things Alistair and Keanu survived would change anyone, for better or for worse. But humans react to perturbations in all kinds of ways.

Alistair knew this better than most. During his time as a prisoner, a slave, a victim of cruelty and torture, he saw men react in all kinds of ways. Many marched into the jungle to die.

But Alistair held on, not simply through force of will —although certainly that was part of it—but also because he approached the profound instability he experienced with a particular perspective.

"Survive the day," he would tell himself each morning. The mantra allowed him to ride the bumpy pockets of air that surrounded him as his life hurdled forward. By the time he was rescued at the end of the war, Alistair had lived through horrendous things. He knew better than most that a single day—a single second—was all it took for a life situation to flip on its head.

One day you're in a crowded, scorching hot, shit-smelling train car. The next, you're building a railroad. You might be taken to a steamship next, then find yourself floating in shark-infested waters.

He never had a guarantee that stability was coming. But he recognized the nuances of instability. Even when turbulence means eating nothing but watery rice for three and a half years, it shifts and changes. If you can survive the day, the next will bring something else—perhaps it will be worse. Perhaps it will be better.

Alistair lived Dr. Hayes's theory—that the most

profound change comes following a period of instability, a period that opens our minds to new ways of thinking, moving, and being.

But what neither of them acknowledged was that this isn't only true of human systems. It's true of the entire universe. The reason comes back to complex systems theory. Within each system—a car, a human being, a society—are potentially infinite subsystems. And as Prigogine noted, the constant churning of all those inter-connected systems is bound to create instability, not as an error or even as an inconvenience, but as a part of the system itself.

Because if systems like humans and societies simply ran as well-oiled machines, there could be no growth. By definition, the system would just repeat itself over and over, everything the same as it ever was.

Nature's open systems get a little wonky from time to time. When the larger system compensates for instability in one area of the system, it necessarily impacts other areas of the system. Rather than grind to a halt, the larger system finds a new means of organization.

That's change.

It's neither wholly linear nor wholly imperfect.

It's simply the way the world works.

CHAPTER 6
WHEREVER YOU GO, THERE YOU ARE

Kevin March can't stand the smell of artificial green apple.

As a child, his parents struggled to maintain steady employment. To make ends meet, his family made their own soap, a combination body wash and shampoo scented with that cloyingly sweet, sickly bright scent that bears very little resemblance to the smell of a fresh Granny Smith.

For Kevin, that smell isn't just the uncanny valley of fruit fragrance.

It's also the smell of instability—the instability of a parent who hides vodka in containers meant for spices and oils. The instability of being repeatedly locked out of his house as a teenager and having to find somewhere else to sleep. The instability of living with his entire family in the back of his dad's semi because they couldn't afford a home. The instability of learning that his father had gone to jail for punching his mother in the face.

And then there was the ultimate instability—the afternoon when he came home from school to find twin restraining orders tacked to the front door.

One had been filed by his father against his mother.

The other had been filed by his mother against his father.

Neither of his parents was anywhere to be found. And, due to the nature of restraining orders, neither would be legally allowed to return to the home.

Despite his aversion to the vodka and the violence and the green apple scent that represented home, it was still home. But he never expected an empty home to become part of the story—especially on the exact day of his eighteenth birthday.

But he was a bright kid, and his hometown of Springfield, Missouri, had a strong public school system. Years before, he'd been smart enough to skip middle school entirely and enroll in ninth grade as a twelve-year-old. He had just experienced a growth spurt, and the gift of height helped him feel more at home among his fifteen-year-old classmates, and helped him befriend his new friend John, a fellow pre-teen in the program who regularly relied on Kevin's height to retrieve items from the top shelf of his locker. Going from sixth-grade spelling exercises to freshman chemistry ended up being too much for Kevin —it would have been too much for most twelve-year-olds! —and before the end of the first year he stepped back to seventh grade. Still, the opportunity introduced him to a new vision for his future. If he applied himself and used his natural intelligence to his advantage, he could build a better life for himself.

Extracurricular activities gave Kevin a welcome outlet, too, and he poured himself into them. He joined a robotics group that gave him his first exciting entry into practical science. And then there was football. A naturally gifted player—and a hard worker willing to put in the hours of conditioning and practice—he excelled on the field. By the time he came home to find those two restraining orders posted on his front door, he was captain of the football team.

Kevin had created a safe, stable environment for himself at school. It had allowed him to flourish, even though his home environment was chaotic at best.

But he was also only eighteen. And now, he was effectively homeless.

It seemed like a no-win situation. But what could he do? He might have slumped against the door and sobbed. He might have called his grandparents in Florida and asked to be taken in.

But he'd always made his own way, and this time would be no different. So when he saw those notices on the door, he went inside, dialed up the internet, and started looking for a job.

GROWING INTO CHANGE

In a single second, Kevin had gone from a high school student with a troubled home life to an independent adult. The notices were, in some ways, simply more of the same. He'd never really known what true stability would look like—that green apple smell still triggered a restlessness in him, a desire to take control of his life rather than wait for his parents to figure out theirs, and that sensation took root when he was very young.

But this was something different. Like a pot of water on the stove, he'd felt the bubbles forming long ago.

Now, his life had boiled over.

Kevin had been as ready for it as a high school senior could be. He'd been dreaming of the day he could strike out on his own and get away from the frustrations of watching his parents seek stability in get-rich-quick schemes. But as prepared as he was, the transition from teenager to adult still felt less like blossoming into the person he was meant to be and more like being thrown into the ocean without a life preserver.

Phase transitions can be misleading in that way.

On one hand, when the switch finally flips—when we finally shift from that bubbling ball of energy into the form we were meant to take—it can feel like a relief. We've survived the flames. We've made it through the awkward in-between-ness that marks the rite of passage from one stage of life to the next.

On the other hand, the instant shift from one form to another is never easy. We suddenly find ourselves in a new world. Like the lanky pre-teen boy Kevin had been when he transitioned from elementary school to ninth grade, we're stuck figuring out how to control our new bodies while we navigate space full of strangers.

We still have to map the terrain of our new life. We still have to figure out how to exist in this new, unchartered place.

The evening his parents filed restraining orders

against one another, Kevin found a job at McDonalds. From that day forward, he got up at dawn and headed to school for conditioning. When the first bell rang, he went to class with the rest of the team. He had football practice after school, with games on Friday nights.

Most days, from 7 p.m. until midnight, he took orders at the fast food restaurant, scraping together just enough money to cover an unfurnished apartment, basic utilities, and the shocking amount of food required to maintain his self-proclaimed "Butterball" physique.

Almost everything in his life had changed overnight.

But he never doubted what he had to do. Knowing that football could be his ticket to a better life, he kept putting one foot in front of the other and, yard by yard, he landed a fully paid financial aid package with Luther College in northeast Iowa.

FROM MILWAUKEE TO NASHVILLE

"I'm sorry, Miss Lee," the woman at the check-in counter said. "But there's not enough room on our docket for your daughter. Can you come back in two weeks?"[1]

A two-week wait was out of the question for the girl's mother. After her daughter had rebelled one too many times, she'd determined that the girl could no longer live in her home. She hoped that the Milwaukee girls' home— a juvenile detention center of sorts—could put her daughter back on the right path.

To the young girl, the situation seemed hopeless. She was certain that life in the home would brand her a troublemaker. And yet, her mother's mind was made up. There was no sense in arguing. So, like it or not, the girl had resigned herself to life as a "bad girl."

But there was no room in the home.

And so, as her mother tried to reason with the woman at the check-in counter, the girl said a silent "thank you" to the forces that had conspired to keep her free. The chance occurrence that would give her one more shot at making a good life for herself.

The girl's childhood had been marked by poverty. For the first six years of her life, she'd lived on a farm with her mother and grandmother. They had very little money, so she was usually dressed in clothes made from spare scraps of fabric. The move to Milwaukee was meant to be a saving grace—an opportunity for her mother, Vernita, to find work. But Vernita's long hours of work returned very little revenue and left the young girl to supervise her little sister, Patricia.

As the troubled child became a troubled teenager, the girl had started acting out. She stole money from her mother and ran away for days at a time. She spent time with older boys—sometimes old enough to count as men —and began to lose interest in school.

Today, these might be spotted as symptoms of a larger problem.

But in the 1960s, her behavior was simply seen as wild. So Vernita elected to turn the girl out of the house. With no available beds at the girls' home, the young teenager was sent to live with her father, Vernon.

Her new life in Nashville proved to be a much more

stable environment than her Milwaukee home. Vernon recognized the girl's obvious intelligence and held high expectations for her academic performance.

But she had a secret.

She was nearly seven months pregnant.

She had tried to hide the pregnancy, growing increasingly aware of how her body was changing—the signs that something big was coming. And shortly after the pregnancy was discovered, the fourteen-year-old went into premature labor. The baby was born weak and ill, and just two weeks later, the little boy died.

What might have happened if she had delivered the baby in Milwaukee? What if just one bed had been open at the girls' home? The secret pregnancy might have been discovered earlier, and the girl might have gotten prenatal care. Maybe she would have been expelled from the school for being pregnant.

Instead, her father was determined to help her turn her life around. Vernon supported her through the ordeal, encouraging her to start over after the baby's death.

And she did.

A few years later, she graduated from high school and landed her first job as a reader for WVOL 1470 radio news. With her "bad girl" past behind her, life looked very different. Her life had changed so much that she might have been unrecognizable, at least on paper, to her Milwaukee family.

The loss of her son had been a tragedy.

But the lack of beds in that Milwaukee girls' home had been another type of catalyst, one that plucked her from an environment where everything seemed impossibly difficult.

There, in spite of the challenges, she found a way to thrive.

RED DOTS, BLUE DOTS, GREEN DOTS, YELLOW DOTS

Imagine you work at a large corporation—the type where hundreds of people serve dozens of jobs with various degrees of difficulty. The workplace is a flurry of energy, a tiny society composed of all types of people.

Most people simply do what's asked of them and not much more. The office couldn't function without them, but they aren't volunteering for any extra assignments.

Then there are the slackers—or, as they were called during my time at GE, "the furniture"—the co-workers who don't seem to do much work at all. They spend much of the day with their feet up on the breakroom table. Some seem to take a ten-minute smoke break for every five minutes of actual work.

At the other end of the spectrum are the high-achievers. For these co-workers, covering for the slackers is almost an Olympic sport.

The department manager needs somebody to come in Saturday morning? They'll be there!

A cross-department committee needs volunteers? They're the first to sign up!

Can someone please clean out the spoiled food in the break room refrigerator? They might crinkle their nose a bit, but if it really needs to be done, they're the first to roll up their sleeves and get to work.

With the slackers and the high-achievers and everyone in between, the company runs essentially the way it should. For every ball one person drops, another is waiting on the rebound. Sure, it would be ideal if everyone pulled an equal amount of weight, but realistically, that's just not the way big corporate machines work.

So imagine if, one day, every high achiever called in sick.

The slackers arrive to find that the weight of the entire company rests on their shoulders.

What would happen next?

Would the slackers step up and take on the work of their hardworking former co-workers?

Or would they continue as they had been, doing less and less until the entire business collapsed in on itself?

It's easy to guess the latter—to assume that slackers are lazy by nature, perhaps even by genetics. If workers like that were left to their own devices, it's hard to imagine they'd do much of anything.

Lazy workers are lazy workers.

High-achievers are high-achievers.

In 2015 researchers at the University of Arizona tested this theory. But they didn't use human workers. They observed colonies of ants.[2]

Led by Dr. Daniel Charbonneau, the researchers built a working ant colony populated with hundreds of tiny workers. To distinguish between the identical bugs, they placed colorful markers on their backs. The high-achievers—the foragers and the groomers—got green and yellow dots, respectively.

Then, there were the wanderers—the ant equivalents of the guys who spend their entire day wandering the office to distract their co-workers with small talk. They got a blue dot.

And then there were the truly lazy ants, technically labeled as "inactive." Researchers marked these ants with a red dot. These ants literally did nothing all day. The colony buzzed around them, as they hung out, relaxing at the outskirts of their little world.

Together, the ants formed a tiny society, cooperating and collaborating to make sure everything was as it should be. The high-achievers picked up the slack. The slackers ate donuts in the break room.

For several weeks, the researchers observed the colony, paying close attention to the various roles. Throughout this time, the ants' roles were stable. Each ant did the same things, day after day.

Until the day Dr. Charbonneau removed the high-achievers.

Like the ant version of the rapture, a human hand reached into the colony and scooped out the top 20 percent of ants. Just like that, the foragers and the groomers—integral parts of a functioning colony—essentially vanished from their little society.[3]

No one had ever performed an experiment like it, so no one—least of all the ants—knew whether the blue- and red-dotted ants would step up to the plate, or simply sip their coffee as the world burned around them.

In the best case scenario, researchers guessed, things

might move forward in sluggish fits and starts. Maybe the colony could sustain itself for the duration of the experiment, but surely things would be much less productive.

In the worst-case scenario, all of the ants would die.

Instead, the colony transformed itself in just days.

By the end of the first week, the inactive ants had taken on the roles of the lost groomers and foragers. They had always been lazy, maybe even assuming that inactivity was in their genes. But when push came to shove—when a catalyst hit, and they were called to adapt—they stepped up to the plate.

Their world suddenly looked very different. But the ants kept marching.

OUT OF THE FRYING PAN

Kevin had only lived in Iowa for about a year when he realized he wanted something different. As much as he excelled on the football field, he knew the NFL wasn't in his future. That realization made him rethink his choice of career paths, which made him rethink his choice of school.

With the sting of green apple in his nose, Kevin once again felt that restlessness in his gut. He'd always had an intense desire to succeed, to build something better for himself. He also knew that, if he wanted better, the path of least resistance wouldn't cut it.

And he knew he was smart. He'd always been an excellent student, and his experiences with the robotics group proved his ability to excel in science.

He couldn't build a career in football, but a degree in

science would open up all kinds of paths. As a native Missourian, he'd grown up hearing about the pre-med program at University of Missouri–Kansas City, UMKC, and while it had seemed out of reach earlier in his life, now he thought it would be a perfect fit.

But there was a problem.

His tuition had been covered by an aid package, and if he moved to Kansas City, that benefit wouldn't follow him. By that point, he'd been paying his own bills for years. But tuition was another beast—there was no way he could stack enough McDonald's shifts to cover tuition and living expenses.

Many of his friends had taken out student loans, but the available loans required a parent to co-sign, and he hadn't really spoken to his parents since he left home.

Fortunately, Kevin was more than just a smart kid and a talented football player. He was also a genuinely good person—people liked him. In a stroke of good luck, a friend's family heard about what he was going through. They decided to bet on his future. They arranged to pay for Kevin's schooling as a personal loan.

Again, Kevin was displaced, but this time, he was in control.

He immediately excelled at UMKC, and by his junior year, he was selected for a research program at Tufts Sackler School of Graduate Biomedical Sciences, where he'd have the chance to work with researchers from neighboring universities MIT and Harvard, an exciting opportunity that was also, admittedly, intimidating. He knew he wouldn't be a red-dot ant, but it was harder to say whether he would be in the top 20 percent—after all, this wasn't just any ant colony. This was where the highest high-achievers went to study.

As it turned out, there was no reason to worry. Like the green-dot ant he'd always been, Kevin poured his entire life into his work in the cancer lab. He'd never done anything halfway, and in truth, he didn't really know how. Some days, he spent countless hours scrubbing mouse skeletons in the lab. Others, he painstakingly entered number after number into master codebooks until his eyes went crossed.

The work was important, and he felt fortunate to be studying at one of the top institutions in the country.

But before long, he began to notice something. His co-workers often went home early. They seemed to be satisfied with "good enough."

At the same time, he reconnected with his friend John —the boy he'd met on his first day in high school, the one who had often invited him to stay over when he was young and looking for anywhere to be but home. The two just happened to be studying at neighboring universities. On a weekend trip, John introduced him to his fraternity brothers, all of whom seemed to buzz with new entrepreneurial ideas.

Like me, Kevin had never considered entrepreneurship. After watching his parents botch money-making idea after money-making idea, he understood better than most how difficult business can be.

But he liked the energy at the fraternity house. No one there seemed content with "good enough."

As it turned out, his connection with John's fraternity was a very good thing. He'd been given tuition money as a personal loan, and now his creditors needed their money back.

Like the student version of *Groundhog Day*, it seemed like Kevin couldn't catch a break. Over and over, he was uprooted and dropped into a new environment. He always excelled, but he never had time to catch his breath.

It seemed like he was always adapting. He never had the chance to restabilize.

In a way, he was well prepared. As someone who had never known stability, he didn't expect much. John offered him a place to sleep on a couch in the frat house, and Kevin was happy to accept. The vast majority of his earnings went to repaying his loan as he kept his nose down and continued to do the best work he could.

In that environment—with the entrepreneurial energy of John and his friends buzzing around him most of the day and night—he couldn't shake the idea that something better was waiting.

And then, John and one of his fraternity brothers approached him. He'd gotten into MIT DeltaV—an accelerator program that would allow them to fast-track their entry into cryptocurrency—and they needed another team member.

The new business venture would be yet another leap. Yet another risk. Yet another upset in a chain of upsets that had marked his entire life—one transition after another after another, with no end in sight.

Kevin jumped at the opportunity.

And this one stuck.

Every new environment had led him to this venture.

Displacement from his family home.

The tuition waiver in Iowa.

A personal loan to attend UMKC.

The fraternity couch.

And now, the pages of *Forbes*, where Kevin and John's company, Floating Point Group, is a leading voice in the exploding world of crypto. According to a 2020 article, the company had "built critical infrastructure to allow cryptocurrency trading at scale between various actors."[4] The two had found a way to monetize Kevin's knack for rolling with the punches by applying it to the changing world economy.

Adaptation can be challenging. But as it turns out, it can be a very good thing.

BLAME THE TABLOIDS

Kevin had faced teenage homelessness.

In a way, so had the young girl. She'd been uprooted from her former life, rejected from the Milwaukee girls' home, and moved across the country. After a childhood of poverty, years of bouncing between homes, and the loss of a child before her twentieth birthday, that girl had shown her ability to adapt to anything life could throw her way.

Just two decades after that fourteen-year-old girl gave birth to a tiny, premature baby, she had grown a media empire worth over fifty million dollars.

By March 1990, when her partner Stedman Graham brought her a copy of the *National Enquirer*, Oprah was one of the most recognized names in popular culture. But as she held that tabloid in her hands, she must have flashed back to what her life might have been.

There, on the cover, was her own photo. Dressed in a vibrant red blazer, the television star flashed a dazzling smile toward the camera. The image was much more flattering than most of the candid shots the *Enquirer* chose to run.

Oprah couldn't have paid much attention to the image. What must have caught her eye was the call-out.

Her Own Sister Tells All.

Below the text, the tabloid had printed three tidy bullet points:

Oprah was Pregnant at 14 and Lost Her Baby
Her Sizzling Romance with a Married Man
The Lies She Told on TV Made Her Mom Cry.

She'd been plucked from Milwaukee. She'd worked her way out of Nashville. She was at the top of her game.

And yet, with every new world came new challenges, as pieces of her former life followed her from location to location, from mindset to mindset, the heavy weight of secrets threatening to topple her success.

If she hadn't already realized it, she must have known it then—life isn't about recovering from our challenges. We're not meant to maintain the same baseline stability for our entire lives.

The challenge—and the beauty—of life is that the transitions are part of the journey. Whether literal or figurative, we don't travel to new places to stay there. We travel *through* our circumstances, growing and changing with each new departure.

We adapt. That adaptation is the point.

Up to that moment, Oprah had never spoken about the baby she'd had as a teenager. But just a few years earlier, she had revealed a related piece of her history in a very special episode of television meant to shine a light on the issue of sexual abuse.

She revealed that she had been raped by a family member as a child. That troubled little girl was not simply troubled. As is often the case, that troubled little girl was, in reality, a victim of an unspeakable crime.

But while she had opened up to the world about one childhood trauma, she'd kept another tightly under wraps.

The reason seems clear enough. Her family had found her pregnancy shameful. They used her teenage promiscuity—a common mechanism for coping with sexual trauma—as a way to blame the young girl for her pregnancy.

It led her to see how not being believed could compound the damage from trauma, and it showed her the power of storytelling.[5] In a way, it was a catalyst for the television show that would catapult her to fame.

Today, Oprah Winfrey is an icon, and it seems as natural to her as if she were born to be on camera. Not only did she build a media empire complete with a magazine, a cable network, a production company, and the highest-rated TV show of its kind, but she has been a profound influence on American culture for over thirty years. Her impact on society is so profound and multifaceted that in 2018, the Smithsonian Museum created a full exhibit dedicated to her life, highlighting a phenomenon called The Oprah Effect, referring to the explosive impact her attention can lend a person, product, or social issue.

But as naturally as Oprah wears the label mogul, she could only achieve it by wading through transformation after transformation. The cruelest circumstances followed her through much of her life—from her childhood sexual abuse to her sister's betrayal to media caricatures that mocked her weight—still, she refused to stop moving.

Long after the *National Enquirer* story lost its public luster, Oprah learned the true origin of the leak. Her sister, Patricia Lloyd, had long struggled with a cocaine addiction. In exchange for the story, the *Enquirer* had paid her $19,000.

Patricia would later die of a cocaine overdose.

Another cruelty in her life's long list.

And yet, Oprah marched on, her eyes firmly on the road ahead.

In many ways, the revelation reshaped her public persona. She'd begun the journey of revealing her past—carefully, of course, and always with purpose—when she publicly described her sexual assault. The next decade would see her career balloon, as she became the daytime voice of strong, confident reason in the lives of so many people who needed her.

Ten years later, she reached a milestone most never reach. Her net worth clocked in at one billion dollars, making her the first Black woman billionaire in United States history. She has won eighteen Daytime Emmy awards, a Tony award, and a Peabody. Her voice is infinitely recognizable, and her image has become one of the most shared memes in digital culture.

It's natural to believe that her life must be easy, but she

still faces challenges. As long as she lives, new struggles will present themselves, and she will have to adapt.

That's true for all of us.

One day, we may find ourselves homeless.

One day, we may experience a shame that feels unbearable.

One day, we may arrive at work to find that 20 percent of our co-workers are gone.

That's the day we adapt to our new circumstances.

ANTS, OPRAH, AND A WHITE GUY FROM MISSOURI

At first glance, it's difficult to find the commonalities between a study on the behaviors of an ant colony, the life of a cryptocurrency pioneer, and the experiences of one of the world's most successful media moguls. The three have little in common beyond their capacity to adapt.

That flexibility was key not only to their success but to their survival.

Struck by catalyst after catalyst, they had no choice but to stay the course, to roll with the many punches until continuous, repeated departures simply became part of the journey. From the outside, this process looks daunting. It probably looked that way from the inside, too.

That's the nature of systems. Any given vantage point only tells part of the story. If we want to understand the whole picture, we have to zoom out.

We have to allow ourselves to travel.

When fourteen-year-old Oprah's premature baby was born, she named the little boy Canaan. The name means "new land, new life."[6] That must have been what Oprah was seeking.

It was certainly what my friend Kevin March wanted when he traveled to New York City to begin his new life, not as the child of poor, struggling parents, but as an up-and-coming entrepreneur with a mind for world-changing technology.

Then COVID-19 struck. NYC effectively closed, and Kevin found himself drawn back to Springfield. There, he rekindled his relationship with his father, and they found new ways to understand one another now that both had transitioned into very different stages of life.

Not long after, his father was killed in a dump truck accident, another catalyst that would shape how Kevin sees the world.

As he reflected on his father's life, he saw something new. His father had shown so much flexibility in his life, the same type of flexibility that had given Kevin a leg up in business. When he left Springfield, he'd known his father as explosive and emotionally immature, as might be expected given that he was very young when Kevin was born. But the father he found when he returned in 2020 had more control over his emotions. He was, in a way, a leader.

It was a poignant reminder that we are all agile, adaptive systems, operating the best we can within the larger system of the universe. We can look at that as a trap—a situation that demonstrates our vulnerability to the elements around us. We can see ourselves as ants, relatively powerlessness should the hand of a scientist reach in to scoop away everyone we've relied on up to that point.

Or we can look at it as an invitation, as confirmation that we can adapt to the new departures life presents.

We don't leave our pasts fully behind us—the scent of green apple might always roil our stomachs, and old family secrets might emerge at inopportune times.

That residue is simply part of growth. It's just one more input in the churning system of life.

PART THREE
LUCK BY DESIGN

CHAPTER 7
THE PURSUIT OF HAPPINESS

n 1978 the *Washington Post* published an article called "The Millionaire's Woe." It would be twenty years before the word *viral* was first applied to a popular news story, but that didn't stop Saundra Saperstein's reporting on lottery winner Robert Bronson from spreading like wildfire.

Bronson had only been twenty-four in 1974 when he won one million dollars from Maryland's state lottery—$6.2 million in today's spending power. Just four years later, his life was, frankly, a mess.

His happy marriage had disintegrated.

He'd been in and out of custody hearings over their children.

He had no idea what he wanted to do for work—after cycling through veterinary school, property management, and entrepreneurship, he told Saperstein that he was waiting to learn whether he'd passed the first test for his real estate license.

It wasn't difficult for Saperstein to make the case that Bronson's life had been all but destroyed by his win.

"I guess I'm happy," he told her. "But I was just as happy...happier, without any money."[1]

Back then, before he became a millionaire, Bronson and his wife had gotten by with very little. He'd even been laid off from his job as a forklift operator just before his big win. Barely scraping by, and with no plan to change things, the family's dread had been growing as they looked ahead to the inevitable expiration of Bronson's unemployment benefits.

Even so, Bronson remembered the past fondly. They'd found a way to be happy despite having relatively little money.

When that big novelty check came through, they hoped that their newfound financial resources would make them even happier.

Instead, it ruined their lives.

The whole thing made for a fantastic human interest story. Readers got to peek inside the lives of lottery winners—of freshly minted millionaires—but instead of a lavish home and caviar with champagne, they found a sad, hopeless, dejected man. The tension between expectation and reality was delicious (well, for everybody except Bronson).

The story would have been a hit in any context. But in a culture that has long delighted in the devastation of lottery winners, it was a hole-in-one.

As early as 1765, people told of the inevitable misery that follows fast on the heels of chance wealth. There's the story of the jackpot winners who were murdered for their money in the mid eighteenth century. In one 1883 story, a businessman struck it rich, but, led astray by his sudden stroke of luck, he invested his money recklessly, losing everything he won and more. And, of course, there's the unfortunate soul who won the lottery, then suffered a heart attack the very next day.[2] The real-life version of Alanis Morrisette's ill-fated gambler actually died sixty-two years before "Ironic" hit the charts in 1996.

Bronson's story was just one more in a long lineage of miserable lottery winners, the type of story that's passed along in taverns, salons, church gatherings, books, articles, and now social media, always with a shake of the head, a smirk, and a healthy dose of schadenfreude.

Over time, the miserable millionaire story—the idea that despair is just a few steps behind a lottery win—has become engrained in our collective psyche. These stories not only offer a big, counterintuitive reveal, they also let us look down on people we might otherwise envy. And, of course, these stories also confirm one of our culture's foundational stories about money—namely, that it can't buy happiness.

There's just one problem.

The conventional wisdom—that lottery winners end up miserable, broke, or dead—simply isn't true. Bronson's story is unfortunate, but according to most research on lottery winners, he's an anomaly. In fact, in one study, the vast majority of lottery winners continued to work in the same job they had before they won. Aside from the increased financial stability, they changed very little about their lives.[3]

Money may not be able to buy happiness. But it's not a recipe for sadness, either.

For some lottery winners, like Bronson and the others featured in most news stories, the energy of that big jackpot tips their lives off-kilter, leaving them floundering.

Others use the money to do, see, and experience things that had always been out of their reach.

And then there are those who do their best to restabilize exactly as they were before their big win.

Like all chance occurrences with potentially outsized effects on our lives' trajectories, winning the lottery is simply an input—an influx of energy that temporarily upsets the systems of our lives.

The real question isn't whether winning the lottery ruins people. The real question is how we, as individuals, restabilize after an unexpected, outsized occurrence.

The real question is what our lives will look like after the dust settles.

THE TURN

The nylon bit into his fingers as Tyler yanked his sneaker laces into a sloppy bow. Still seething about his most recent loss at the poker table, he yanked on a running jacket. He didn't even bother to stretch. He just hit the ground running, his feet pounding the Las Vegas concrete as he set out to burn off some of his rage.

With each steady, even tap on the pavement, the numbers flashed red through his mind.

$4,539 lost that day.

$2,127 the day before.

$918 the day before that.

He blew out a long, intentional breath. That was just the way things went sometimes. Logically, and, as the expression goes, you can't win 'em all. He'd been playing professionally for long enough to know that, intimately, in his bones.

Still, with each new loss, his body seemed to ache just a little more. He hated that feeling, of being tense and angry and sore, jaw locked and stomach clenched.

Lately, he wasn't sure the rush of a win made up for the despair of a string of losses. But at least winning allowed him to blow off some steam. With his wallet fat, he could afford to spend the early morning hours partying, surrounded by that euphoric buzz of people who love you. He could almost forget that those people only loved him because they were partying, and when you get that high and drunk, you love everything.

To drown out the thoughts that had become more and more intrusive, he put in his earbuds, hit shuffle on his iPod, and clipped the device to his tank top.

He hoped to hear something hard and fast to push him through his run. Instead, he was greeted by a gentle acoustic guitar riff and soft, pure voices, cooing something about lifting up their hands.

What the...?!

He slowed to a loping stop and looked at his iPod. The words "Holy is the Lord" scrolled across the tiny pixelated screen. Right on cue, Tyler rolled his eyes and clicked the iPod forward to the next song.

The tinny opening riff of Tupac's "Keep Ya Head Up"

filled his ear buds, and within a few strides, Tyler found his rhythm.

Even with the music there to distract him, his mind drifted to dark thoughts.

His life had been so good—a dream, really—for a long time. Just a few months before his twenty-first birthday, he'd put sixty dollars into an online poker site. Within six months, he had turned that sixty dollars into over six figures. He dropped out of college, and shifted his focus to poker and partying, traveling back and forth between Vegas and home. Young, wealthy, and talented, he had everything he ever wanted. His beautiful wife was the cherry on top of his dream life.

Of course, not everyone saw his life as a dream. His parents worried, often asking gentle questions about his lifestyle and encouraging Tyler to take time out for church.

Tyler scoffed at the idea, sure that the last thing he needed was God. He didn't begrudge anyone the crutch they needed—he certainly had his own crutches—but the idea of sitting in a stuffy church pew after a night of shutting down the clubs sounded, frankly, stupid.

He was making stacks of money and partying with friends all over the world. What more could God possibly have to offer?

Then came the call.

In between games at the World Series of Poker, Tyler took a call from back home.

His wife was leaving him for someone else.

It was like being kicked in the stomach by a horse.

His life suddenly and unexpectedly tilted on its axis,

he tried to reset it, to keep everything as close as possible to his normal routine. He moved to Chicago and threw himself into the nightclub scene. Even more than before, the drinks and dancing and partying felt frantic. Almost panicky.

And in the quiet, gray, early hours of the morning, when he had no way to distract himself, he would cry himself to sleep.

Like a rat trying to pull itself out of a flooding sewer, Tyler clung to anything that could pull him just a little higher, even as he felt himself slipping.

Dangerously. Irreparably.

He'd asked for a lot of things in his life. Mostly, he'd gotten them. Mostly, they hadn't lived up to his expectations, at least not in any long-term way.

But as his mind drifted back to the randomness of hearing a Christian song—a song he would never have loaded onto his iPod himself—he wondered whether that moment might be something he'd asked for, quietly, secretly, as he cried himself to sleep one night. This was, after all, in the age before Spotify. His device wasn't connected to the internet, so there was no way some random contemporary Christian song should have been on his device. And with a thousand songs to shuffle through, the odds of that song popping up were steeper than many he'd faced at the poker table.

Unless...

No. The thought was dumb. He shook it off, and picked up his stride.

HITTING THE JACKPOT

Psychologists tell us that not all happiness is created equal.

Namely, research into the brain science of happiness distinguishes between the quick, easy lift of a funny video and the long-term, hard-earned satisfaction of accomplishing a goal.

The former is all about pure, physical gratification—the type of joy we feel when we eat delicious food, pull on a soft piece of clothing, or step into a warm shower. This type of happiness is called *hedonic* pleasure. While that term is often associated with physical gratification—typically sex—it applies to any situation that gives us pleasure through physical sensation.

By nature, hedonic pleasure is short-lived. The tenth bite of that perfectly cooked steak never tastes as good as the first. The softest cashmere sweater can start to feel a little itchy by mid-afternoon. And while we might stay in the shower until the water runs cold—aside from the ice bath believers, who doesn't love a long, luxurious shower? —you can't bottle those first few seconds of warm comfort.

Hedonic pleasure isn't built to last.

Or, more accurately, our bodies aren't made to enjoy it for any extended period of time.

There's a scientific reason that hedonic pleasure fades. The same adaptability that helps humans overcome challenges, adjust to new circumstances, and experience new things also short-circuits our ability to extend hedonic pleasure through a process called hedonic adaptation.

First introduced in the 1950s, the concept of hedonic adaptation explains why those intensely pleasurable moments fade so quickly. Our brains process the rush of good feelings and respond by helping us acclimate to the situation. Once we adjust to the hit of pleasure, it doesn't feel nearly as enjoyable.

Our brain's powerful ability to adapt kills our buzz.

But understanding the brain's ability to adjust to pleasure isn't just an interesting bit of trivia for your next cocktail party. When we understand the fleeting patterns of hedonic pleasure, we're better equipped to pursue more lasting forms of happiness in addition to the quick, temporary pleasures of hedonism.

That's where eudaemonic happiness comes in. Eudaemonic happiness is the type of joy that comes from pursuing fulfillment—the joy of watching your kid perform in a school concert or the pride of delivering a big presentation at work. Eudaemonism emphasizes a deeper sense of well-being and fulfillment that comes from living a meaningful life. It's characterized by a sense of purpose, self-actualization, and personal growth.

That last aspect of the definition—the personal growth part—is key to understanding why the path to fulfillment is never a straight line. Since eudaemonic happiness requires us to do something purposeful and fulfilling, it's almost always preceded by less enjoyable periods. Before you could watch your kid stand up and sing "Three Blind Mice," you had to get through the months of sleepless nights with an infant. Before you could blow that presentation out of the water, you had to struggle through learning a new topic and skill set.

Without those more challenging periods, the pleasurable periods wouldn't be nearly so fulfilling. The challenge feeds the reward.

And the reward is sizable. Compared with the surge of hedonic pleasure—which stays relatively isolated in the mesolimbic dopamine system—the joy we get from eudaemonic happiness actually impacts the pre-frontal cortex,[4] the part of our brain that helps us regulate our thoughts and emotions.

As psychology research has progressed, scientists have realized that it's not only hedonic pleasure that relies on dopamine for its punch. *All* pleasure is related to dopamine.[5] Accordingly, all pleasure fades.

This is why, even when we experience major, life-changing events—winning the lottery, for instance—the burst of joy we feel eventually ebbs, returning us to what scientists call the happiness set point. When the dopamine wears off, we naturally feel less joyful than when the hormone first flooded our brains.

Although neuroscience has made huge strides in explaining the brain chemistry behind pleasure, social scientists have been studying happiness for decades. Around the time the lottery ruined Robert Bronson's life, a team of researchers studied people just like him.

The resulting study is not-so-subtly subtitled "Is Happiness Relative?"

Driven, in part, by the popular conversations about miserable millionaires, Brickman, Coates, and Janoff-Bulman set out to interview people who had won large sums in the lottery within the past year, asking them to rate how much they enjoyed a series of everyday activities:

talking with a friend
watching television
eating breakfast
hearing a funny joke
getting a compliment
reading a magazine

These activities all fit beneath the umbrella of hedonism, as each is a simple, sensory joy unrelated to major life goals. Researchers wondered whether the massive surge of excitement brought on by winning the lottery would dull participants' senses to everyday pleasures.

And to some degree, it did.

On average, their lottery-winning participants rated these everyday activities as slightly less pleasurable than a control group of non-winners. But while the difference was statistically significant, it was also relatively minor—the average score for a lottery winner was 3.33 on a 5-point scale, while non-winners scored these activities at 3.82. Their hedonic pleasure—or at least their self-report of their hedonic pleasure—appeared to have decreased by around 13 percent, an effect researchers guessed was the result of ongoing and cumulative hedonic adaptation.

The incredible dopamine spike they'd experienced when they learned that they were millionaires had, apparently, reduced their ability to take pleasure from life's ordinary things.

And yet, the winners were happy with their lives. In fact, when they were asked to rate their current, pre-win, and future anticipated happiness, lottery winners scored higher than the control group. They also reported being happier at the time of the study than they had been before their win.

Of course, that's not *always* the case. There are plenty of people who wind up miserable after a win. Robert Bronson was one.

Tyler Todt was another.

KNOW WHEN TO FOLD 'EM

As Tyler rounded the corner, bound for the last leg of his run, he felt tired. Not physically tired, the way we might expect during a hard workout, but a deeper sense of exhaustion.

He'd spent years desperately trying to fill the hole left by his divorce, piling more and more excess into every day and every night. All that excess came with a hefty price tag, but his success at the poker table meant he didn't have to think much about that. During his years as a professional gambler, he'd racked up over seven figures in winnings. But he still felt crushingly sad.

Colby, a friend he met at a bar, gave him a gentle nudge towards doing something different—inviting him to come lift weights with him the next morning at 5 a.m. Tyler went along with the idea. And he found that the goal-oriented weight-lifting community gave him a new, refreshing kind of focus.

More than that, the people he met inspired him in a different kind of way. Before, he'd been driven to achieve wealth and luxury. Now, he saw people who were driven toward a sense of calm and peace that seemed to be largely unrelated to material wealth.

At that thought, he'd reached out to a family friend he had always admired. Eddie was a pastor of a large church, and was thrilled to make time to have coffee with Tyler. And before Tyler knew it, he was asking Eddie every tough question in the book.

Why does God allow bad things to happen?

How do you make sense of the hypocrisy of so many so-called believers?

Does God really care if people drink and party?

With a sense of humble confidence, Eddie answered each of Tyler's questions, urging him to ask the same questions of himself. He didn't have all the answers, of course—that's why it's called "faith," he explained—and while Tyler wasn't fully ready to accept Eddie's answers, he found the pastor's responses compelling.

They decided to have coffee again. And again. And again.

After several meetings, Eddie presented Tyler with a challenge. He told Tyler to pray for a sign from God every morning for a month. Tyler still wasn't sure there was anything of faith he needed in his life, but he also knew something had to change. He was willing to try the experiment.

That morning, before he laced up his sneakers—before he'd even headed down to the poker table—he'd prayed for the thirtieth time.

God, if you're up there, show yourself to me. Show me something.

But Tyler wasn't focused on that now. Now, he was determined to finish his run as strong as he'd started it. So he leaned into the music on his iPod.

With one last, bold declaration, Tupac repeated the song's tag line, sending Tyler into that chilly familiar silence, and for a moment, he was alone with his thoughts and the steady pounding of his running shoes.

Then came the gentle acoustic guitar riff.

The first time, he'd been irritated.

Now, he recognized the moment for what it was.

Once again, he slowed to a stop, but this time, he let the music play. Tears in his eyes, he staggered to a nearby bench and sat.

He'd been playing the odds for a long time, but this felt different. This felt a little like winning the lottery.

ANTS ON A LOG

Jane Goodall felt the same way.

Observing from a distance, she watched as David Greybeard sat back on his haunches. His back was arched and his expression was one of pure concentration as he peered into the ant hill. Occasionally, he stuck a big, leathery finger into the colony, sometimes retrieving a tiny insect and bringing it to his mouth.

Goodall wondered whether he'd spotted her— whether he was listening for her now-familiar movements or watching for the flash of her tawny blonde ponytail.

She knew the chimpanzee well by then, and he knew her. She'd named him David when she first arrived on the trip. Jane has often joked that she loved animals from the moment she "popped out of the womb" in 1934.[6]

At the age of ten, she'd become infatuated with the

story of Tarzan, the man who lived among the apes, joking even 89 years later that Tarzan married the wrong Jane.

Around that time, she was gifted a stuffed chimpanzee, which she named Jubilee, after the first chimpanzee born in the London zoo.

But when Jane came of age in the early 1950s, there were few women in any field of science, animal studies included. In general, traditional educational paths weren't accessible to women, at least not to the extent that they are now, so the odds of Jane Goodall becoming Jane Goodall were exceptionally low.

Until December 1956, when Jane opened the post box to find a letter from her school friend Marie-Claude Mange.

Marie-Claude's family had acquired a farm outside of Nairobi in Kenya. Knowing that Jane had always wanted to experience the jungles of Africa—spaces rich with the powerful animals she loved—Marie-Claude invited her friend to visit.

All Jane had to do was find the money.

Up until that day, Jane had been working as a secretary, a respectable job for a woman at the time and generally following the same steps into adulthood that many intelligent and independent-leaning women were taking. For most, dropping everything in London to travel to a distant shore with uncertain prospects for employment or security would be unthinkable.

But Jane didn't hesitate. She'd always known what she wanted. She didn't need another sign to know it was time.

She quit her secretarial job and took on double shifts waiting tables to earn enough for the voyage, and by

March of 1957, she was aboard the *Kenya Castle*, a ship bound for Nairobi.

As she wrote in a letter home, "I <u>still</u> find it difficult to believe that I am on my way to <u>Africa</u>. That is the thing—AFRICA. It is easy to imagine I am going for a long sea voyage, but not that names like Mombasa, Nairobi, South Kinangop, Nakuru, etc., are going to become reality."

The ship arrived on April 3, Jane's twenty-third birthday, and she added her first impression of Africa to the end of her ship's log letter home.

"It's so wild, uncultivated, primitive, mad, exciting, unpredictable...I am living in the Africa I have always longed for, always felt stirring in my blood."[7]

For Jane, the trip itself was like winning the lottery. And with more destinations than she could possibly visit, she settled on exploring what she could explore on her limited budget.

So when she was introduced to Dr. Louis Leakey, a paleontologist in need of a secretary, she saw an incredible opportunity.

Dr. Leakey wanted a skilled secretary who was willing to travel across Africa.

Jane fit the bill.

The job would become much more than a job. Dr. Leakey soon mentored Jane through writing her first grant —a request to the Wilke Foundation to fund an expedition to Tanzania. She would be part of a trio of young women—the trimates, as they called themselves—determined to study apes in the wild.

Jane would study chimpanzees. Birute Galdikas would study orangutans. And Dian Fossey would study gorillas.[8]

And so it happened that a young woman without a college degree would observe David Greybeard in a landmark moment in science. That day, as she watched, David plucked a few long stalks of grass from the ground, twisting them together to fashion a stiff probe. His head cocked to one side, he stuck the grass into the mound's entrance and watched as the ants marched in a neat line up the stalk. One by one, they filed on to the grass until, in one strong, steady move, David brought the stalk to his mouth and dragged his tongue along it.

It wasn't pure chance. After all, she'd pursued her dreams tenaciously, following through on every opportunity that presented itself.

But that moment and all those that followed—as she first approached David, offered him food, and finally realized they were communicating with one another—were "very, very special."[9] As she would later say of the many life-changing experiences she had while observing her chimpanzee companions, it was "an amazing story that unfolded by amazing luck."[10]

KNOW WHEN TO WALK AWAY

The definition of luck is "to come upon something desirable by chance."[11] Objectively speaking, luck is something external to us.

But there's another piece of the puzzle, one that gets lost in so many everyday conversations about luck: if we're not open to the role of chance in dramatically changing our lives, we can easily overlook the possibilities presented by serendipity.

Maybe it's no coincidence that chance is a synonym for opportunity.

There's a scientific explanation for the necessary interaction of luck and natural design—the collision of our external circumstances with our internal drive. Since humans are open systems, we can't help but take in energy from our surrounding environment. The very definition of an open system requires that we constantly exchange energy and matter with our environments, adapting and adjusting along the way.

By nature, we take in the energy around us. And by nature, we sometimes take in too much.

This is the heart of Prigogine's theory of dissipative structures—when systems are overwhelmed by excess energy, they must release that energy somehow. And as I've written in previous chapters, that process typically results in some kind of systemic reorganization.

As open systems, humans continually face tipping points. These moments of excess energy—whether we interpret that energy as positive or negative—overwhelm our systems, and our lives are forced to reorganize, one way or the other.

When Tyler heard that song for the second time, he took it as a sign. I can't weigh in on whether that song was God's voice or simply Tyler's mother loading the song onto his iPod in a clever attempt to steer him to a healthier life trajectory. Either way, it was the last straw in a life that was slowly falling apart.

For years, Tyler's life had been flooded with extra energy—the frantic parties, the volatile poker table, the women and the drinks and the pain. That song was the tipping point, the moment when he released the built-up energy and allowed his life to reorganize.

Unlike Jane, he'd fought against openness. He'd spent his twenties gritting his teeth and running against the wind. As the excess of his life threatened to overtake him, he pushed back harder and harder, unaware that there is no fighting nature.

When we reach a tipping point, there's no turning back. Our system *will* reorganize. The only choice we have is *how*.

Tyler was finally ready to make that choice for himself.

He started to attend church on Sundays and formed friendships and a community through his newfound faith. Eventually he met his second wife at that church. And while there were highs and lows during the next several years—years he called his "half-in, half-out" period—his identity gradually shifted from the dopamine junkie he'd been before to an ambitious, goals-oriented leader, eager to share his experiences with others.

In a single second, his entire perspective changed. In a single second, he discovered a path to true happiness. In a single second, he got off the hedonic treadmill.

TOOLS

Jane didn't have to wait for chance to knock twice. She immediately recognized the significance of the observation.

All her life, Jane had rejected what she had been told —that animals didn't have complex inner lives or emotions. She'd seen her dog, Rusty, express emotions. And she'd even watched birds and squirrels relate to one another as they flitted between London's trees.

But her observations had been anecdotal and difficult to prove.

Until now.

Now, she'd seen David do something that no animal had done before, at least not in human presence. He'd crafted a tool.

As elated as Jane was with her finding, it was difficult to convince others of its validity. So she kept watching. Later that same year, she watched with wonder as a group of apes sucked the moisture out of clumps of leaves, using the dried debris as a sponge for soaking up water. Doing so allowed them to clear the liquid from hollowed logs, making insects and other treats much easier for the apes to retrieve.

And then she saw those same apes teach the trick to their children.

As Dr. Leakey would note, the finding was significant: "Now we must redefine tool, redefine man, or accept chimpanzees as human."[12]

In many ways, Jane had already chosen the latter option. She'd notably refused to follow the traditional habits of scientific researchers, assigning the chimpanzees names rather than numbers. Using alliteration to group families—Fifi, Freud, and Frodo in one family, Goblin, Gremlin, and Glitter in another—she observed the apes as though they *were* human, bringing an openness to her observations that allowed her to make some of the most crucial discoveries of the twentieth century.

The noteworthiness of her openness stretches far beyond her research methods, though. Had she not been open to a seemingly random invitation to travel from London to Africa, she would never have met David Greybeard. She would never have learned to write a research grant. She would never have changed the way we understand human evolution.

It might have happened that the little ape-loving girl who played with earthworms and loved all things wild simply grew up to be a London woman who loved trips to the countryside and books about wilder places.

Except that Jane was always watching for her chance. So when it appeared, she recognized it for what it was—a lucky break, ready to be incorporated into her life's trajectory.

KNOW WHEN TO RUN

I believe many people resist the type of openness that brought Jane Goodall to Africa because they're afraid. Some are afraid of the financial implications of trying something new. Some fear for their physical health and safety if they explore other parts of the world, fears that have not borne out in my experiences around the globe. Some are afraid of being judged by others as irresponsible or stupid.

And some are simply afraid of who they might become. I think they recognize that changing their lives will change who they are on a fundamental level. They fear becoming someone they don't recognize, because even though that change might leave them more fulfilled, they worry that it could also leave them less happy.

Fortunately, science tells us that this is unlikely.

In their study on lottery winners, Brickman, Coates, and Janoff-Bulman also interviewed a third set of participants—people who had been in an accident that left them paralyzed. At the time of the study, many of these participants lived in full-time rehabilitation centers, so we might expect them to rate their happiness level a bit lower than usual. And this hunch holds up—on a scale of 1 to 5, they rated their happiness at just under 3 points.

It's not surprising that this group would rate their overall happiness as significantly lower than lottery winners.

What *is* surprising is how all three groups rated their anticipated future happiness—the winners anticipated a score of 4.2, the control group averaged 4.14, and the accident victims 4.32.

The scores were statistically similar for all three groups.

As it turns out, what might seem like our brain's buzzkill is actually a safety guard—we're hardwired to return to a baseline level, whether that means coming down from the high of a very pleasurable experience or regaining our balance after a devastating loss.

That's the beauty of the hedonic treadmill.

Sure, it cuts short the joy of a poker-table win.

But it also reassures us that we don't have to remain in a bad place for long. If we lean into our natural ability to adjust, adapt, and realign, it's only a matter of time before we move through the difficult times and into a new, potentially stronger, form.

That means we can try new things with the reassurance that failure is only temporary.

It means we can take reasonable risks, confident that even the worst-case scenario eventually leads us back to our baseline.

It means we can go on a trip to Africa, even with nothing in particular waiting for us, and know that eventually we'll adapt. In the meantime, we'll take in amazing experiences. We'll learn new things. Yes, we'll encounter very difficult challenges, too, but the hedonic treadmill means we can embrace them without fear.

In fact, it means we *must* embrace these new experiences if we want to have a more substantial, less shakable form of happiness. Because unlike hedonic pleasure, which only provides us with a short-term dopamine spike, eudaemonic happiness is much more stable and consistent.

We only reach eudaemonic happiness when we play the long game, pursuing not fleeting happiness but the kinds of things that give our lives purpose.

CHAPTER 8
POST-TRAUMATIC GROWTH

I n the 1950s a petite man taught the classics at Gresham's private boarding school in Norfolk, England. Most days, he dressed in a tweed jacket and a conservative tie, the stereotype of his profession and field personified.

But where his dress might give the impression of a bumbling, scattered professor, the thirty-something World War II veteran moved slowly and carefully as he navigated the campus, ever mindful of the effect strenuous activities had on him.

On a typical day, he might be greeted by a star student as he approached the podium. A thoughtful pupil might bring him a pitcher of water and a glass. Another might grab the megaphone he used to overcome his increasingly raspy voice.

The professor was known for his in-depth lectures on things like the daily lives of Pompeiians in the days before the volcano as well as the standard fare of Latin vocabulary drills and lessons on properly conjugating verbs.

Often, his lectures were peppered with hacking, desperate coughs. And as the decade wore on, he relied more and more on the megaphone to reach the students in the back of the classroom.

He had loved what he did once. But years earlier, he felt himself falling out of love with the profession. The professor had long dreamed of leading a more creative life. He enjoyed craftsmanship—working with his hands to design and realize something new and interesting.

So, unbeknownst to his students, the professor had been in talks to join BBC television, which was going through a major boom. He had discovered his passion in the work of creating puppets for the school's production of Aristophanes' *The Frogs*, and that work had been appealing to the network.

Now he was presented with the opportunity to help create something big—he would be a founding member of a nationally recognized televised theatre group.

It was an incredible opportunity, but one that he needed to carefully consider—after all, while it would be an extension of his longtime love of the classics, it would also be a very different application. It would mean leaving behind academic life and his identity as a lecturer. It would mean becoming someone fundamentally different.

It could change his life for the better, but it was easier to stay where he was, relatively happy and relatively stable. So he had pressed on with his work at the school, even as his health deteriorated. Any major creative endeavors would have to wait. The timing just wasn't right. In the meantime, he would fit small tastes of creativity in between the requirements of his teaching job.

But eventually even that work had been put on hold as he squeezed lectures, grading, and student meetings in between visits to his doctors in London. Those trips left him with horrendous dark-red circles on his chest and back, an expected but unpleasant outcome of the treatment he hoped might save his life. Doctors and scientists had been researching possible cures for lung cancer for over a century by that point, but the treatment was still rudimentary at the time. At only forty-three years old, the relatively young man succumbed to the disease.

The professor left behind a wife and three children. His salary had barely been sufficient for the treatment regimen, and the family had very little savings after his passing, certainly not enough to continue his sons' schooling at the private school.

Fortunately, Gresham's offered the widow and her children a gift—they would allow the boys to finish their education free of charge through their graduation. It was the least they could do for the family of a loyal faculty member.

For the school's part, this decision would prove to be a wise investment. Nearly seventy years later, one of the teacher's sons, billionaire James Dyson, returned to Gresham's and gave a speech about the impact of his father's tragic death on his life. He donated over eighteen million dollars to the school in order to help them build a new science and engineering wing, a gift that married Dyson's life's work in innovation and technology with that of his father's work in the classroom.

On the day the building opened, James climbed a

short stack of stairs to speak to Gresham's students. He wore a suit, like his father had, but James's clothing was sleek and sharp material, boasting a bold red collar that stood in bold contrast to the late professor's more conservative attire.

"When I sat where you are," he advised the class of 2022, "I thought experience was important...I now know the opposite to be true. Be curious. Throw yourself into everything....Look out for guardian angels."[1]

James Dyson has written and spoken frequently about the impact losing his father had on his life. Only nine years old when his father passed, he was left feeling alone and bereft of a fatherly guide, just as he was entering crucial years of his development. As he wrote in his first autobiography, *Against the Odds*, "It made me feel like an underdog, someone who was always going to have things taken away from him. It made me feel that I was alone in the world—which inevitably, in better moments, will also make a small boy feel special. I had no one to help me through my boyish problems, and no one to cite his own youthful experiences as an example to when I thought I might be troubled by something that no one else had ever been through before. Life became something I had to make up as I went along, and I had to work everything out for myself. In crass, psychoanalytic terms, I suppose it made me a fighter."[2]

The loss of his father instilled James with equal parts drive and fear—he had much to overcome but little support in a world he knew well could be random at best, cruel at worst.

At first, he sought advice not from those immediately around him, but from books. He devoured the stories of the best and brightest in a variety of fields, searching for someone to emulate—someone who had embraced everything life had to offer. Someone who was the absolute best at what they did, but who continued to push themselves anyway.

In high school, he took up running. True to form, he shrugged off his coach's advice, instead seeking out books by the best runners in the world. This advice led him to the Winterton sand dunes. At six in the morning and again at ten o'clock at night, James raced up and down the dunes.

And, unsurprisingly, he quickly surpassed his school's top runners.

It was a thrilling discovery and one that would guide his life's work—by simply embracing *different*, he could propel past those who focused on *best*. The approach was rebellious by design, and it led him to later describe his boyhood self as a "misfit," and a "stubborn, opinionated child," but it also helped shape the entire trajectory of his life.

He'd come out of one of the most traumatic experiences a child could have. But it wasn't the trauma that shaped him. It was his *response* to the trauma.

In searching for a mentor—someone to fill the gap he'd imagined his dad would fill—he'd found a system.

And he was determined to use that system to follow his dreams. He would not repeat his father's mistakes, putting off his dreams until, inevitably, it was too late. He made a promise to himself not to wait to do the work he loved.

Though James would not follow his father into classical studies, echoes of his father's passion have reverberated through his life. First in books and later through personal relationships, he surrounded himself with men he admired and emulated—his "personal pantheon," he called them. He studied the work and personal philosophies of men like Isambard Kingdom Brunel, a nineteenth-century giant of engineering and industry. James saw not only scientific brilliance in his work, but artistic beauty. In the curves and math-informed structures of Brunel's bridges and designs, he saw that remaining as close as possible to the "pure function of the object" could produce a simple and timeless form of beauty.

In 1970 Dyson reached out to Jeremy Fry, engineer and British businessman, seeking advice and financial support in one of his early project ideas. To Dyson, Fry's unconventional manner made him a modern-day Brunel. He craved more guidance outside the strictures of his design school, whose formalist and prescriptive methods frustrated him. He remembered what he had learned from long-distance running: to be better, be different.

Fry didn't agree to fund Dyson's idea, instead offering him a job at his company Rotork, the company that would give James the framework to found his own company. There, he dove into his work as a designer and engineer, plunging himself into skill sets from welding to hydrodynamic design—if he needed it to execute his vision, he was ready and willing to learn.

Later, James would develop his own company, one where he would think about ordinary, overlooked machines differently. His signature design would marry form and function in a way that elevated the simple household tool to a work of art.

That tool, of course, was Dyson's first revolutionary vacuum cleaner.

His work is in millions of homes across the globe. His innovative, ambitious approach to his work speaks to his mindset. Since childhood, Dyson refused to settle for relatively happy and relatively stable.

And we can easily trace that approach back to a single moment—the moment his father died.

AT SEA

What would you say if you were asked to name the worst thing that's ever happened to you? Would you be able to name just one event? Could you think of a single, specific occurrence?

Think of it now.

Did it shift the way you thought about your identity?

As you were going through that terrible experience, did you wonder whether you were capable of responding effectively to the situation?

If you answered "yes" or "probably" to either question, your experience can scientifically be classified as a crisis.

That would be enough to qualify you as a participant for a major, grant-funded study on the sociology of crisis. One such study was undertaken by Florida State University professors John R. Reynolds and R. Jay Turner.

During the course of their project, they asked over fifteen hundred participants these questions.

The study was a major stepping stone in our understanding of crisis theory, an approach at the intersection of psychology and sociology that offers a compelling framework to understand how experiences like James Dyson's—the most harrowing, earth-shattering, traumas that leave us shaken to our cores—can actually result in improved mental health outcomes.

These experiences, scientists argue, are about more than just our brains. They're about the relationship between individuals and their environments, and how major, sudden shifts in our social context result in similar changes within our psyches.

To understand crisis theory, imagine yourself on a boat that's being tossed around a stormy, turbulent sea—one that's not so different from the one Alistair Urquhart survived. But even knowing Alistair's story—even knowing that humans have survived being stranded in the ocean—you shudder at the troubling amount of water accumulating at your feet as waves crash against the sides of the boat. You cling to the boat, but only with the terrible knowledge that the entire vessel might sink, taking you with it.

If you've never been on a boat before, you'll likely feel terrified—any potential enjoyment is out the window as you cling to your life jacket and try to keep those hard seltzers down. The more the boat rocks, the more upset you'd become. The threat would feel existential.

Where the thought of drowning was once a distant possibility, the experience of sailing through a major storm crystalizes that threat, redefining your relationship with the outside world.

An experience like that easily qualifies as a crisis.

But if you're Captain Ahab, the storm might bring you to life. Rather than feeling afraid, you might drag your peg leg up to the bow and shout for Peleg to bring you your harpoon (and none of this seltzer business—bring the man a hearty flask of grog!).

When your entire life is the sea, one little storm won't mean much—unless it results in an additional catastrophe, it certainly won't make you rethink your relationship to the water. You've likely already done that, the first time you sailed through a major storm.

This is the utility of crisis theory for psychologists—if we can understand why and how some people turn crises into fortitude, we can better treat those whose crises result in depression, anxiety, and a host of other mental health issues.

To get to the heart of the matter, Reynolds and Turner asked participants one more set of questions:

Did the experience show you that you can handle things that you never thought you could handle?

And if it were to happen again, do you think you could handle it with less difficulty?

Some participants answered no. These participants reported continuing psychological effects from the experiences—in many ways, they were still living in the time of crisis. They hadn't yet found a way to make sense of what they'd experienced, and as a result, they tended to fit the clinical criteria for depression and anxiety.

Those who answered yes, on the other hand, showed

consistently higher self-esteem—and this effect was amplified by how devastating the crisis was.

In other words, participants who had survived events that rocked their world—terrible things like witnessing a murder or experiencing assault with a weapon—saw significant boosts in their self-esteem, *but only if they were able to move on*.

If we can resolve the crisis, overcoming the experience in a way that allows us to look back on the chapter as meaningful but closed, we can reap enormous benefits. We can experience higher self-worth, a greater sense of self-efficacy and resiliency, and improved outcomes for long-term mental health. In fact, these crises can even build up exponentially, so that those who experience more than their fair share can emerge stronger and stronger—Ahab marching around the bow of a sinking ship—and crucially, less beaten down by their bad fortune.

The key isn't the crisis itself.

The key is what happens next.

WHEN GRIEF IS AMBIGUOUS

My friend Stephanie's life was, she thought, exactly how she designed it to be.

She had earned a master's degree in public policy.

She had built a successful and fulfilling career as a leader in nonprofit work.

And she had found a loving and devoted husband.

As Stephanie and her husband approached twenty years as a couple—just shy of eighteen years of marriage—things weren't always perfect, but she felt happy with the life she had created for herself. She felt comfortable in her own skin.

On a Tuesday afternoon that was more or less exactly like every other Tuesday afternoon she'd lived for the past decade, she realized she needed to print something. For an unknown reason, her laptop refused to print, so—she borrowed her husband's.

Stephanie would later reflect on that moment—a clear catalyst—from a different vantage point. She'd built a new life with a new career and a new way of approaching the world. From that new perspective, she would call that moment "an activating event." She would estimate, eventually, that more than 90 percent of the population would experience something like it in their lifetimes. She would build a thought empire around the concept and use it to help tens of thousands of people like her.

But that ordinary Tuesday, that term didn't yet exist.

All she could think about was that terrifying, stomach-lurching moment when a roller coaster reaches the top of its tracks. And then it falls.

Around her, her home looked the same. No earthquake had shattered it to pieces. On the surface, all was as it should be.

But Stephanie's relationship to that home seemed to have dissolved in an instant. She had been "launched... into a new reality."[3]

This sense of being lost in unfamiliar waters is common among those who have recently lost loved ones. We all understand, if only hypothetically at first, the pain of surviving the death of someone close to us. Sometimes, we see the death coming, as when Alec Dyson succumbed to cancer.

Other times, the loss is instant.

Regardless of how the loss unfolds, we have tools to process this type of grief, including collective, formal ceremonies like burials and remembrance services. This process is common to every culture and society, and although the grief can be overwhelming, there is some comfort in knowing that it is very much a shared, communal experience.

There is a clear intention to the ways we, as a society, mark the deaths of our community members—we come together to collectively process the experience of loss so that we can resolve our grief and move forward together.

But sometimes we lose loved ones not through the finite end point of death, but through processes that are much less collective—and rarely ritualized.

That Tuesday, when Stephanie opened her husband's laptop, an email notification appeared, confirming a renewed subscription to a dating website.

She clicked the email open, unaware that she was pulling a thread that would completely unravel her life as she knew it.

She confronted her husband, hoping for some reassurance.

But it never came, and the more she pulled that thread, the more she learned. Over the next days and weeks, she uncovered a web of affairs, some of which appeared to be new and ongoing, others stretching years into the past and long ended. All of which had been ongoing while she believed she was in a loving and committed marriage.

As Reynolds and Turner might ask, *Did the experience cause you to wonder whether you were really the person you thought you were?*

Did it cause you to be uncertain of whether you were capable of responding effectively to the situation?

Faced with a crisis she could barely fathom, Stephanie stumbled forward. She'd been plunged into a dark tunnel, and as she scrambled around in the pitch black nightmare, she slowly but surely realized that this chapter of her life had been slammed shut.

It was a loss—a grief she'd never experienced before—but it wasn't so finite as a death. There were no ceremonies to lay the matter to rest. No community would gather graveside to share their condolences. No one would recognize her as a widow, though she says "that's what I imagined it felt like."

She would have to find her way through on her own.

In the months after Stephanie's discovery, the world seemed to turn upside down. She scrambled for a foothold even as she felt angry, black waves lapping at her ankles.

Her first instinct was to restabilize, to claw her way back to the familiar territory of her loving marriage, her stable home life, her established career.

She tried to understand.

She started therapy.

She tried to keep things under wraps, fearful that if word got out, there would be no going back.

There were bad days and worse days. A better day

here and there. Days that felt numb. Others that felt fiery and piercing.

And soon it became clear—there would be no restabilizing, at least not in the way she'd hoped. Her life had reached its tipping point, and her life as she knew it was gone. With nothing to return to, there was nowhere to go but forward.

After the inevitable divorce, Stephanie's grief continued. She sought help for coping with the pain she felt, hoping for a community to grieve with. But this wasn't the typical type of grief—there was no body to bury and no funeral to plan. And nobody in the world seemed to understand what she was going through.

How could she mourn someone who still lived?

For the next several years, she worked with therapists to process her trauma until, eventually, her life found new stability. In working through her grief, things looked different from that vantage point—with her newfound distance, she had a gained a deeper understanding of what she'd been through in the context of human experience. So she began to write about what she had learned.

And suddenly, she wasn't so alone. She met others who experienced different kinds of loss and expanded her definition of what it meant to experience loss—people whose loved ones were living with Alzheimer's, people who had been abandoned, people whose spouses were in prison. All had gone through the process of grieving someone who wasn't quite gone, of being plunged into a situation where a comfortable, well-worn identity suddenly clashed with reality.

And now Stephanie had gone through the process,

too. Now, through the hard work of healing, she had successfully reconciled her most traumatic crisis.

Something happens when we're forced to redefine our lives—who we are within our social environment. Our old assumptions—who we are, what we do, where we live— no longer fit us. It's like putting on an old sweater, but where the garment used to feel cozy and warm, now it feels itchy. Was that stain there the last time you wore it? Were the sleeves always so short?

Stripping off that old, scratchy sweater gave Stephanie space to explore who she wanted to be. As a kid, she'd loved to write. In fact, she had once shared her dream of becoming a published author, boldly declaring her future the ways kids do.

Back then, she'd been told that she would never make a living as a writer. The comment was made casually, an offhand remark the near-stranger had probably made a dozen times. But it made an impression on Stephanie. As she grew up, she heard similar sentiments about starving artists and out-of-work creatives, and that was that.

She wanted to be successful. So she put aside her love of writing.

But as she carved out a new post-divorce identity for herself, she felt drawn to write. She felt drawn to share her experiences—to help others through her story.

Eventually, Stephanie partnered with Dr. Sophia Caudle to explore and research the psychology of her experience. Together, the two women co-authored the *ambiguous grief process model.*

She rediscovered that childhood desire to be a writer, and when she looked at that dream through new eyes, she realized it was her true calling. Though her 2022 book, *Soulbroken*, (which won Gold in the Nautilus Book Awards, Grief and Loss category) she found a way to connect with others, building a community of support for people facing various types of ambiguous grief.

The aftermath of opening that laptop had shattered many of Stephanie's preconceived notions about grief, but her experience was about more than that—what she'd been through showed her how life can change in an instant.

What we really need in the shadow of grief isn't a somber funeral or a refrigerator full of casseroles. Those things help, of course, but only in the way they move us closer to the real goal.

What matters in times of suffering isn't how the world reacts to us—it's how *we* react to the *world*.

THE EMOTION EQUATION

It would be easy to misunderstand crisis theory as trite, even a little Pollyanna-ish—it can come across as an echo of well-meaning family friends in a funeral receiving line.

Things are always darkest before the dawn.

The universe won't throw you anything you can't handle.

Everything happens for a reason.

These misguided oversimplifications couldn't be further from the purpose of this chapter or crisis theory more generally.

In reality, the psychology of crisis is far from sunny. When crises hit, we're knocked out of our comfort zones and into the radically unstable world of critical fluctuations—the frantic zigzag of a heart monitor, but without the reassuringly steady rhythm.

As Reynolds and Turner warn, the positive effects of overcoming a crisis are only activated if we *resolve* that crisis. That's a hopeful finding for those who make it to the other side of a traumatic event.

But for those who don't find resolution, a crisis experience closely predicts major periods of depression and other mental health struggles.

This doesn't always look like ambiguous grief—as I've noted throughout this book, change is rarely as linear as that might imply.

Instead, as a recent study led by award-winning psychologist Robert Klein made clear, many people who fail to resolve crises do so not out of an inability to overcome but rather because they refuse to acknowledge the crisis at all.

Klein's team calls this situation *defensive denial*. Defensive denial takes many forms—from cynical jokes to a casual shrug of the shoulders—but its core is always the same. People use defensive denial to avoid their emotions, and when we refuse to feel our emotions, we pay for it with our overall mental health.

We very rarely choose to face crises, and we never choose to encounter catalysts. But when they occur, we have the power to choose our response.

This might look like scouring the library for books when we lack the guidance of a father figure.

It might look like couples therapy and divorce and months of in-depth study on our experiences.

As long as we accept our grief, there is no right or

wrong way to experience a major crisis event. The important thing is that we embrace the emotional impact and ride the turbulence through to the other side.

Because, very often, something even better is waiting for us.

CHAPTER 9
THE SCIENCE OF
SERENDIPITY

I t was a dark and stormy night, and a team of frazzle-haired scientists huddled around a diabolical experiment. At the center of it all was a tiny body, completely at the mercy of a team of Godlike lab technicians bent on its demise.

A crack of ominous thunder rang out as their subject teetered on the edge of survival.

Illuminated by the flash of lightning through the windows of the laboratory, the scientists started their dastardly work, removing the little being's genes, one by one, until he was nothing more than a shell of the bacterium he once was.

Cue: maniacal laughter.

This account of a groundbreaking study in experimental evolution is only partially fictionalized—I have no idea what the weather was like as the Indiana University scientists engineered the little being into near-oblivion. And the study's lead author, Dr. Moger-Reischer, seems like a perfectly nice guy—not at all reminiscent of Dr.

Frankenstein—unless he's hiding his true evil scientist identity behind a perfectly normal scientific bio.

But this much is true: the organism at the center of their study, Mycoplasma mycoides JCVI-syn3B—Mike for short—was in for a rough ride. Dr. Moger-Reischer had robbed the bacterial cell of every single gene that wasn't absolutely essential to his survival.

While I doubt it was any consolation to Mike, the team had a very good reason for doing so, one that had nothing to do with malice or mischief. They did it to continue their work in experimental evolution, an overall program of research that uses model organisms to study the processes of natural selection. In a highly controlled lab setting, environmental circumstances can be manipulated to dramatically speed up a species' evolution. This allows research teams to test evolutionary theories that would otherwise be impossible to observe.

In Mike's case, the team wanted to determine whether a stripped-down cell would survive and reproduce, and if it did, what the evolutionary results would be.

From Mike's perspective, this must have seemed so random. Why him? Why then? To what end?

There were no clear answers to these questions on the researchers' side, either, at least not the type of answers that might offer some reassurance to the struggling being. There was nothing particularly special about Mike. The timing wasn't personal, either—the experiment was just one piece of the researchers' programs of study.

And by definition, no one knows how an experiment like this will end. Mike might thrive. Or he might die. The latter looked at least as likely as the former. Scientists evaluate the health of bacteria like Mike using a measure called fitness. A compiled score of seven smaller evaluations, the measure accounts for things like growth rate, antibiotic resistance, and competitive interactions (essentially how well the type of bacteria is expected to perform in a cage match with other bacteria).

Key to this particular experiment, the measure also includes genetic diversity, or the variety of genetic traits and characteristics within a species. This factor is so important to bacterial fitness because the survival of any species is essentially a numbers game. Inevitably, some genetic combinations will not lend themselves well to thriving in a particular environment. As a result, the organisms with those genetic combinations don't typically survive long enough to reproduce. The stronger combinations, on the other hand, pass their traits on to future generations, resulting in a stronger overall species.

As the research team explained, species with more genes should, in theory, be better suited to adapt to their environment. Those with fewer aren't expected to thrive.

When the Indiana University team finished modifying Mike, he had only 493 genes, a number that stood in stark contrast to the 20,000 genes in humans and 7,500 in the largest bacteria. With so little genetic diversity, the team explained, the little bacterium's odds of thriving were low.

That, along with other measures of fitness, predicted a bleak future for Mike. On a scale of 0–100, with 100 being completely healthy and 0 being, well, dead, the bacterial cell scored a 50 on the fitness exam.

Up until the moment when the scientists began stripping away Mike's genes, the cell *could* have lived a perfectly normal life. Perhaps that life wouldn't have been quite as exciting, but he could have settled into content-ment, whatever that might look like for a bacterial cell.

But there was nothing he could do to change the past. His missing genes were gone forever.

Through no fault of his own, Mike was fighting for his life.

WHEN IT'S TOO FAR TO WALK

Mike faced enormous constraints.

I, on the other hand, was ready to embrace the freedom that comes with being a twenty-something single guy with very few responsibilities.

In the spring of 2012, I had quit my job at a Fortune 500 to prepare for my move to Rio, but I still had over a month before I would leave for Brazil. An old friend of mine invited me to hitchhike with him around the south-eastern United States.

It would be a new experience for me, but Garrett was an old hand at finding rides and exploring the country this way. For him, it had started as a way of hitting out-of-town football games and grew into a natural part of his of life. I probably wouldn't have ventured out to do this on my own, but with Garrett as experienced company, the opportunity far outweighed the risk.

There is a unique freedom in hitchhiking. By nature, it forces you to relinquish control of your environment. I wanted to explore what might happen if I leaned into the random unpredictability of a trip like this.

The experience did not disappoint!

I saw places I likely never would have thought to travel. I met people I likely wouldn't have crossed paths with. When we set out on our journey, we had a handful of destinations in mind. We wanted to see the world's tallest waterfall east of the Mississippi, hike the Fiery Gizzard trail, visit Western Carolina University, scamper up the Indian staircase, and possibly do a stint on the Appalachian Trail.

There are so many beautiful places in between that it didn't really matter how exactly we got from place to place. We just had to figure it out as we went based on the taillights that happened to veer over to the side of the highway.

But the most eye-opening part of the experience was the glimpse it gave me into human psychology.

I was stunned at the frequency at which people offered us money, and how generous people were with their time and gas. I vividly recall a van full of African American women who slowed down beside us, rolled down their windows, called out "God Bless!" and threw money at us. We would have refused the cash—we weren't broke, we just needed a ride—but they drove away before we had a chance.

We heard a lot of people's stories on that journey, many of them marked with twists and turns and highs and lows.

Though it may seem counterintuitive to some, letting go of the exact path you take, putting it in the hands of the opportunities that come your way, is freeing. It allows you to appreciate the journey as part of the destination.

The most interesting aspect was how often people

took us exactly where we wanted to go, even if it was well out of their way. I'm not sure this was always a good thing —some of the most interesting things happened when we had to follow the random pathways ahead, truly going along for the ride with a total stranger.

One of those rides took us to the town of London, Kentucky, en route to Eastern Kentucky University to visit a friend of Garrett's. We wrote "Richmond"—the college town where the university is located—on a big flat of cardboard with a fat, black permanent marker. I held one corner of the sign, and my friend Garrett held the other, waving at traffic and hoping for a lift.

About half an hour later, a boxy wood-paneled station wagon slowed to a stop, and a man about our age with a bushy black beard and a gregarious grin leaned out the car window.

"Hey, guys! Where ya headed?" he asked in a thick Kentucky accent.

With literal rose-colored glasses perched on his nose, the guy looked like a rugged American version of Paul McCartney. His energy was infectious.

"Heading in the general direction of Richmond," I replied. "How about you?"

"Sweet! That's exactly where I'm going," he continued, not even hesitating long enough for us to answer his question. "What's y'all's names?"

"This is Garrett," I replied, gesturing toward my friend. "I'm Adam."

He looked at Garrett, amused. "Really? Garrett? With two R's and two T's?"

"Yup," Garrett confirmed.

"Me, too," the driver laughed. "Hop on in."

We chucked our backpacks and cardboard sign in the back of his car and were off to wherever this guy decided to take us.

A few hours later we found ourselves in Richmond, where driver-Garrett was visiting a few buddies. Several of them sat on the porch, nursing beers.

"Where y'all from?" one asked, curious or suspicious, as Garrett and I crawled out of the station wagon with our big hitching backpacks in tow.

Driver-Garrett answered for us. "They're Kansas boys! I picked 'em up hitchin'."

Without missing a beat, our new friends nodded and handed us a couple of cold PBRs. "Any friend of Garrett's is a friend of ours."

That night, we crashed on the floor of the backyard guest house.

Some might have called it a risk to invite complete strangers to sleep in their guest house. After all, we were two random, smelly, unkempt dudes. The most they knew of us was that their friend picked us up along the side of the highway.

But the group was friendly and welcoming. Mostly, they just wanted to have a good time.

The next day, driver-Garrett dropped us off on the side of another on-ramp so we could continue our adventure.

He pointed to my friend with a grin. "Two R's, two T's!"

The Garretts laughed again and hugged as I pulled our packs out of the car. We exchanged social media accounts and followed each other, promising to stay in touch in that way that feels good at the time but doesn't usually pan out.

I didn't think about driver-Garrett for several months. During the two weeks after we met, friend-Garrett and I continued to trek across the American Southeast. We hiked part of the Appalachian Trail and stood at the foot of the tallest waterfall east of the Mississippi, meeting so many incredible people along our route. It was a fantastic way to spend the weeks before I packed up and left for Rio.

Nearly a year later, and having not thought about driver-Garrett since we hopped out of his station wagon so many months ago, I started to see more of his social media posts. They were fascinating, and I looked forward to them every week. His videos and pictures were like a window into a totally different kind of life.

He and his friends would gather around bonfires, playing bluegrass expertly on their banjos. They even had a guy who held a bona-fide washboard between his knees, providing that percussive accompaniment not often heard outside Appalachia.

As I scrolled social media one evening, one of their videos caught my eye. I clicked "share" and sent it along to my sister, sure she would appreciate the group's down-to-earth vibe.

"These are the guys I was telling you about!" I wrote. With that, I hit send and kept on scrolling.

BUCKLE UP

When I think of Ralph Nader, I don't typically think about what we have in common. But throughout his college years, he did his fair share of trekking down the side of the highway, thumb out and sign in hand, just as Garrett and I had done.

"I never took the train out of Princeton the whole time I was there, except maybe once," he shared. "By hitchhiking, I met all kinds of people—everyone from doctors to truck drivers. It was one of the greatest educations in the world."[1]

He traveled tens of thousands of miles this way. When he visited home on weekends, he hitched. When he wanted a quick getaway, he hitched. Sometimes he even cut class to hitchhike to field research sites, where he explored Native American issues, the plights of migrant workers, and the lives of those who worked primarily on the road.[2]

What he learned through hitchhiking often informed his academic and journalistic projects, including several essays on the mental health issues among disenfranchised Native Americans.

Hitchhiking, with all its unpredictability, opened Nader up to experiences and observations that he could not possibly have predicted or chosen.

One thing he witnessed would change shake him so deeply that it would change his life—and the trajectory of the American automotive industry.

While he was attending Harvard Law, he often hitch-hiked a familiar path between Boston and his Connecticut home. On one such trip, the driver rounded a bend and came to a hard stop. Ahead of them lay a tangled mass of smoking metal, multiple cars twisted and mangled into what was obviously a tragic collision.

Since the emergency vehicles were yet to arrive on the scene, the driver pulled over, and he and Ralph approached the wreckage, hoping to help where they could. Neither was sure what they would find inside the cars. It was obvious there would be injuries, but impossible to know how bad.

Nader had been through this before. As an avid hitchhiker, he'd come across many accidents—no one can hitchhike thousands of miles without seeing the good, the bad, and the ugly of highway travel. He'd seen people thrown from cars. Some cars had burned to a crisp, the drivers still inside. He'd seen limbs crushed and mangled and heard similar stories from the truckers he rode with.

In the back of his mind, he had often questioned car design. Safety seemed strangely low on the priority list for car and truck manufacturers, and he'd wondered what could be done to pressure car manufacturers into investing in safer systems.

But other concerns had taken priority in his mind.

Until that day.

As he and the driver approached the multi-car collision, he strategically approached a car that seemed a little less damaged. The passengers of that vehicle, perhaps, had the best odds of surviving, so it made sense to focus on them first.

The gruesome scene inside that car changed him forever.

On the front seat lay the body of a little girl. During the collision, she had apparently been thrown forward just as the glove compartment's latch had popped open.

"The glove box door worked like a guillotine on that little girl," Nader would say of the incident many years later. "That got me to begin looking more seriously at the issue of auto safety."

At the time, car accidents—from minor to deadly—were considered the responsibility of the drivers. The car industry took no responsibility for safety, blaming injured motorists for being overly reckless or incompetent.

But a little girl decapitated by one of the car's cosmetic features flew in the face of this logic, and it was too tragic for the young man to ignore.

Shortly after, in 1965, Nader published his book *Unsafe at Any Speed: The Designed-In Dangers of the American Automobile*. He pulled no punches, giving a controversial, hard-lined critique of the automotive industry. "For over half a century the automobile has brought death, injury and the most inestimable sorrow and deprivation to millions of people," he wrote, his righteous anger driven by the unnecessary death of a little girl he'd never met.

Nader's aggressive brand of idealism didn't always make him a popular character in politics and business, but his activism undeniably reimagined the auto industry. In September 1966—just ten months after his book was released—President Lyndon B. Johnson signed the National Traffic and Motor Vehicle Safety Act into law. The act created an agency to enforce new and updated vehicle safety standards and supervise safety recalls.

He had no control over the things he experienced on the road, and he couldn't force the car industry to change.

The only power he had was over his own responses. And, as it turned out, that power was more than enough.

RIPPLE EFFECTS

Mike knew a little something about power, too. But in his case, it was his lack of power that was most striking. A "minimal cell," he was completely at the mercy of researchers and his environment.

He was faced with two options.

He could give in. Succumb to having most of his genetic identity stripped away. Who could blame him? Certainly not the scientists, who had low expectations for his survival and reproduction.

Or he could fight. He could do everything in his power to survive and thrive against all odds.

His predicament was unexpected and out of his control. But his *reaction* was not.

And Mike had a lot to fight for. It wasn't just *his* survival at stake—it was his entire lineage. If he could survive, he could begin the evolutionary process of spawning stronger, better, versions of himself—cells that would continue to grow and improve and make a massive contribution to the scientific understanding of evolution.

Of course, bacterial cells don't really *fight*, so to speak. They simply exist within their environments.

And yet, from an outside perspective, Mike seemed to be quite a fighter! Even though he had been cut down to the bare minimum, he showed no signs of giving up.

The little cell happily produced a new generation of bacteria. To the team's surprise, that generation produced their own offspring, and those offspring reproduced, too. Suddenly, Mike's family tree was huge!

For nearly a year—two thousand generations of bacterial reproduction—Mike's descendants continued to grow in Dr. Lennon's lab. The cells proliferated rapidly, but they remained about the same size as Mike, a runt by design. It looked like the cell had passed along his weakness to his children. The result wasn't entirely surprising or even disappointing to the scientists. After all, they hadn't really expected him to survive at all, let alone procreate!

But from visual cues alone, they had no way of knowing whether the new cells continued to be as weak as their ancestor or whether they had defied the odds and begun to evolve into stronger, more robust organisms. The only way to test these new cells' fitness was to put them into different environments with different species under different circumstances.

This would be the ultimate test. Their ancestor had weighed in at just 50 percent fit. Would the youngest of the cells be even weaker?

The result was a resounding *no*.

As it turned out, the bacteria's genetic make-up had evolved rapidly—strikingly so. The new cells had evolved so completely that they scored 100 percent in their fitness test, double Mike's score at the beginning of the experiment. In less than a year, the species had evolved so much that the genetically weakened cells had completely caught up with their unaltered cousins.

As it turns out, "life really does...uh...find a way."[3]

The study was published in *Nature*, the top scientific journal in the world, and was praised as a groundbreaking discovery for evolutionary science.

Mike had stared down a catalyst more profound than you or I could ever imagine. He survived. But in a way, his own survival was the least important part of the experiment. Because Mike's survival created a ripple effect. The catalyst he experienced had a profound experience on Mike, his descendants, the researchers, and the entire world's knowledge of scientific truth.

It wasn't about luck. It wasn't even about making the most of your situation, although Mike certainly did that.

It was about leveraging a catalyst toward a greater good, something every single one of us can do, no matter how small or stripped down we feel. When we find ourselves at rock bottom, staring down a future we don't even want to imagine, we have no choice but to act on the catalysts we experience. And that's no less true when we experience catalysts we think of as positive—things like winning the lottery or being in the right place at the right time.

The choices we make in response to catalysts are larger than any single event, person, family, or even species, because we're all a part of the systems that surround us.

Sometimes, we're like Mike, fighting to survive long enough to build a better life for our families.

Other times, we're like Nader, fighting for safety and justice for those well beyond our immediate social circles.

One truth is constant. Whether we realize it or not, the way we choose to respond to seemingly random catalysts has the power to shift the catalysts others will experience. We never choose our catalysts. But we choose how to respond.

And those responses have the potential to reshape the entire world.

Years after my adventure in Kentucky, I held up that same cardboard sign that Garrett and I had held on the side of the road as we waited for a ride to Richmond.

The sign was a little worse for wear, but I looked decidedly better, or at least I like to think so. I wasn't ragged and unwashed. I wasn't lugging a pack on my back.

This time, I wore a suit with a silk tie and a white boutonniere. Next to me, driver-Garrett still rocked his bushy beard, groomed a bit more carefully for the occasion.

And next to him stood his wife, my sister Reghan.

ON SERENDIPITY

After I sent my sister Garrett's video, she followed him on social media. They began to exchange messages and eventually started to date long-distance. I spoke at their wedding, where I shared how happy I was to welcome Garrett into the family—who better to marry your sister than a person so kind that he wouldn't hesitate to pick up a couple of hitchhikers and put them up for a night?

It all happened like dominoes, one catalyst leading to another which led to another. The entire system shifted because my brother-in-law happened to drive down the highway where friend-Garrett and I stood. I was standing there because an old friend had invited me, but also because I had a month before I would start my new job in Brazil. I'd found that job through a random conversation with a family friend, after a random conversation with an executive at my previous job made me realize I wanted something different.

Catalyst-response,   catalyst-response,   catalyst-response.

With each shift, the system of my life changed for the better. But that benefit pales in comparison to the larger picture. My sister met the love of her life. My family added a new member. And a new life, my nephew, eventually came into this world.

From a systems perspective, Nader's story isn't so different. Because he happened to enjoy hitchhiking, because a random truck driver spotted him on the side of the road, because a driver lost control which happened to cause a deadly accident, and because it was Nader who happened to approach a car whose interior was too grisly to ignore, millions of people's lives changed.

It's easy to call these moments coincidences. And technically, they are.

But each of these moments—these catalysts—are the result of the choices others made in response to their own catalysts. We can track down some of them if we search hard enough. Most will never reveal themselves. They blend into the fabric of the universe.

Catalysts can shake you to your core. They make you question who you are, what your values are, and what you want to do with your life. These moments are part and parcel of being a human on this planet. By their very nature, catalysts come when we least expect them. All we can do is take the pieces we have left—minus those that have been radically altered by a moment completely out of our control—and find a way to become the next version of ourselves.

The stories I've told in this book are stories of random chance. A random meeting at a bank. A random conversation with a mentor. A random experience at a music camp. A random song on your iPod or a wartime fabric shortage.

When we hear these stories, they seem so incredibly random.

And in a way, they are.

It's just that randomness isn't the exception—it's the rule. These random, chance occurrences are the very fabric of our existence, the spark that snowballed into the first signs of life, that resulted in the incredible coincidence of our births, that brought you to this book and this day and this life.

We can call it luck or serendipity or random chance. But no matter what we call it, one thing is clear.

Catalysts are beyond our control.

So we might as well enjoy the ride.

NOTES

1. CHOOSE YOUR OWN ADVENTURE

1. "Oprah Talks to Charlize Theron," *O Magazine*, November 2005, https://www.oprah.com/omagazine/oprah-interviews-charlize-theron/all.
2. Lynn Hirschberg, "Charlize Angel," *New York Times*, February 24, 2008, https://www.nytimes.com/2008/02/24/style/tmagazine/24coverlynn.html.
3. Melvin Lerner, *The Belief in a Just World: A Fundamental Delusion* (Springer, 1980).
4. Nassim Nicholas Taleb, *The Black Swan: The Impact of the Highly Improbable* (Penguin, 2008).
5. National Weather Service, "How Dangerous Is Lightning?" https://www.weather.gov/safety/lightning-odds.
6. "Oprah Talks to Charlize Theron," *O Magazine*, November 2005, https://www.oprah.com/omagazine/oprah-interviews-charlize-theron/all.

2. THE MOMENT EVERYTHING CHANGED

1. United Nations, "Justice and Reparations Still Critical, 30 Years on from Sarajevo Siege," *United Nations News*, April 6, 2022, https://news.un.org/en/story/2022/04/1115742.
2. Zain-Ul-Abideen Ahmad, "Self-Report Measures and the Replication Crisis," *The EDIT Lab Blog*, December 9, 2020, https://blogs.kcl.ac.uk/editlab/2020/12/09/self-report-measures-and-the-replication-crisis/.
3. Norman R. Brown, Peter J. Lee, Mirna Krslak, Frederick G. Conrad, Tia G. B. Hansen, Jelena Havelka, and John R. Reddon, "Living in History: How War, Terrorism, and Natural Disaster Affect the

Organization of Autobiographical Memory," *Psychological Science* 20, no. 4 (April 2009), p. 403, emphasis mine.

4. Turkeys are slaughtered at 5 to 6 months, but to maintain the impact of Taleb's striking example, I hope you'll suspend your disbelief at this arbitrary timeline.

5. "Disaster at Last Befalls Capt. Smith," *New York Times*, Tuesday 16th April 1912, ref: #3315, published July 30, 2004, https://www.encyclopedia-titanica.org/disaster-at-last-befalls-capt-smith.html.

3. YOU POKE THE BEAR

1. While I won't discuss closed systems in this book beyond this footnote, a closed system is simply a system that does not give and take with its environment—imagine, for example, a hermetically sealed vault or, more simply, an airtight container. Since energy and matter cannot pass into or out of closed systems, they technically cannot create ripple effects in the larger systems around them, so they aren't particularly relevant to this book's topic.

2. In a parallel I find fascinating, Archduke Ferdinand was assassinated in Sarajevo, the same city that would later become a war zone and, even later, play host to the memory experiment I described in the previous chapter.

3. Incidentally, Gabrielle would become an early adopter of the "bob" hairstyle, a style that would become iconic in the 1920s because so many women adopted it.

4. People understand the original catalyst in all kinds of ways—some call it God, some call it cosmic energy, some call it random chance. The point is not to explain what that catalyst was, a question I'll leave to the reader, but rather to explain the process. Because that same processes are still at work in everything around us, including our lives.

4. THE BOILING POINT

1. Merlijn Olthof, Fred Hasselman, Guido Strunk, Marieke van Rooij, Benjamin Aas, Marieke A. Helmich, Günter Schiepek, and Anna Lichtwarck-Aschoff, "Critical Fluctuations as an Early-Warning Signal for Sudden Gains and Losses in Patients Receiving

Psychotherapy for Mood Disorders," *Clinical Psychological Science* 8, no. 1 (2020): 25–35, https://doi.org/10.1177/2167702619865969.

2. Pun very much intended.

3. Kunhardt Film Foundation, "Condoleezza Rice Interview: Discovering a Passion for International Politics," YouTube video, 36:11, May 9, 2023, https://www.youtube.com/watch?v=0IET3kefd9A.

4. Interestingly, she still continued to play, holding musical events in her DC apartment.

5. SOME MINOR TURBULENCE

1. Commercial air travel is actually one of the safest forms of travel, statistically, with only one fatality per 3.2 million passengers. You are more likely to be injured riding a bike (around one in 3,300), driving car (around one in 100), or even crossing a city street (one in 550). But that's not what our brains tell us when our plane starts to lurch through a windy sky.

   IATA, "IATA Releases 2021 Airline Safety Performance," press release, March 2, 2022, https://www.iata.org/en/pressroom/2022-releases/2022-03-02-01' National Safety Council, "Bicycle Deaths," https://injuryfacts.nsc.org/home-and-community/safety-topics/bicycle-deaths/; National Safety Council, "Odds of Dying," https://injuryfacts.nsc.org/all-injuries/preventable-death-overview/odds-of-dying/.

2. Alistair Urquhart, *The Forgotten Highlander: An Incredible WWII Story of Survival in the Pacific*, 1st ed. (Skyhorse, November 1, 2011), p. 233.

3. Alistair Urquhart, *The Forgotten Highlander: An Incredible WWII Story of Survival in the Pacific*, 1st ed. (Skyhorse, November 1, 2011), p. 144.

4. Alistair Urquhart, *The Forgotten Highlander: An Incredible WWII Story of Survival in the Pacific*, 1st ed. (Skyhorse, November 1, 2011), p. 224.

5. Alex Li San, "Keanu Reeves: A Life Story That Will Inspire You," *Introverts Digest*, May 14, 2020, Medium, https://medium.com/introverts-digest/keanu-reeves-a-life-story-that-will-inspire-you-c6cd361d05ea.

6. In his autobiography, Alistair credits his ability to survive to his time in the Boy Scouts.

7. Alistair Urquhart, *The Forgotten Highlander: An Incredible WWII Story of Survival in the Pacific*, 1st ed. (Skyhorse, November 1, 2011), p. 242.

8. Dr. Mathieson's treatment for infection was to send the patient to the latrines to retrieve a handful of maggots. The patient was to count the maggots, then place them on the wound where they would eat the necrotic flesh. Once the wound was clean, the maggots would all need to be removed (hence counting them) so that they would not continue to damage healthy tissue.

9. Alistair Urquhart, *The Forgotten Highlander: An Incredible WWII Story of Survival in the Pacific*, 1st ed. (Skyhorse, November 1, 2011), p. 252.

10. Alistair Urquhart, *The Forgotten Highlander: An Incredible WWII Story of Survival in the Pacific*, 1st ed. (Skyhorse, November 1, 2011), p. 5.

11. Genevieve Hassan, "Keanu Reeves' Ode to Happiness," BBC News, June 22, 2011, https://www.bbc.com/news/entertainment-arts-13838742.

6. WHEREVER YOU GO, THERE YOU ARE

1. "Oprah's Teen Pregnancy Leads to a Second Chance," aired on October 19, 2011, on OWN.

2. Daniel Charbonneau, Takao Sasaki, and Anna Dornhaus, "Who Needs 'Lazy' Workers? Inactive Workers Act as a 'Reserve' Labor Force Replacing Active Workers, but Inactive Workers Are Not Replaced When They Are Removed," *PLOS One*, September 6, 2017, https://doi.org/10.1371/journal.pone.0184074.

3. No ants were harmed in the writing of this book, although I can't speak for Charbonneau's lab.

4. Frederick Daso, "Floating Point Group, an MIT Crypto Fintech Startup, Modernizes Digital Currency Trading," *Forbes*, April 13, 2020, https://www.forbes.com/sites/frederickdaso/2020/04/13/floating-point-group-an-mit-crypto-fintech-startup-modernizes-digital-currency-trading/.

5. Oprah Daily, "Finding the Right Therapist," https://www.oprahdaily.com/life/health/a37577404/finding-the-right-therapist/.

6. Lauren Porter, "Oprah Reveals Name of Son She Lost at Age 14," *Essence*, October 27, 2020, https://www.essence.com/news/oprah-

reveals-name-son-she-lost-age-14/.

7. THE PURSUIT OF HAPPINESS

1. Saundra Saperstein, "Millionaires' Woe," *Washington Post*, August 16, 1978, https://www.washingtonpost.com/archive/local/1978/08/16/millionaires-woe/bf93baef-198a-4a11-baae-abe0938ff4ec/.
2. Jonathan D. Cohen, "Why the Myth of the Miserable Lottery Winner Just Won't Die," *Slate*, July 30, 2022, https://slate.com/human-interest/2022/07/mega-millions-jackpot-winner-numbers-myths-about-lotteries.html.
3. Jonathan D. Cohen, "Why the Myth of the Miserable Lottery Winner Just Won't Die," *Slate*, July 30, 2022, https://slate.com/human-interest/2022/07/mega-millions-jackpot-winner-numbers-myths-about-lotteries.html.
4. Pamela A. Jackson, M. Joseph Sirgy, and Gabriel D. Medley, "Neurobiology of Well-Being," in *Research Anthology on Mental Health Stigma, Education, and Treatment*, ed. Information Resources Management Association (Hershey, PA: IGI Global, 2021), 32–52, https://doi.org/10.4018/978-1-7998-8544-3.ch003.
5. The functions of dopamine are incredibly complex, and neuroscientists learn new things about the hormone every day. While I focus on its relationship with pleasure in this chapter, that is only one aspect of dopamine's role in our bodies.
6. "Dr. Jane Goodall on Living with Chimps, Their Language & the Possibility of Bigfoot," *Jimmy Kimmel Live*, YouTube video, April 14, 2023, 9:03, https://www.youtube.com/watch?v=_cS3BAoGwWM.
7. Jane Goodall, *Africa in My Blood: An Autobiography in Letters: The Early Years*, ed. Dale Peterson (Mariner Books Classics, 2001).
8. Caitlin Starowicz, "Louis Leakey Selected Three Women to Study the Great Apes, They Inspire Others Today," *CBC*, https://www.cbc.ca/natureofthings/features/louis-leakey-selected-three-women-to-study-the-great-apes-they-inspire-youn.
9. "Dr. Jane Goodall on Her First Encounter with David Greybeard at the Women's Equality Summit," The Passionistas Project Pop Culture Passionistas, YouTube video, https://www.youtube.com/watch?v=BG6hU9FVqxU.
10. Susan Karlin, "Jane Goodall on the Amazing Story of 'Chimpanzee,'" Fast Company, April 17, 2012, https://www.fastcompany.-

com/1680549/jane-goodall-on-the-amazing-story-of-chimpanzee.

11. Merriam-Webster, s.v. "luck," accessed December 20, 2023, https://www.merriam-webster.com/dictionary/luck.

12. Renuka Surujnarain, "Now We Must Redefine Man, or Accept Chimpanzees as...Humans?" *Jane Goodall's Good for All News*, July 24, 2019, https://news.janegoodall.org/2019/07/24/now-we-must-redefine-man-or-accept-chimpanzees-ashumans/.

8. POST-TRAUMATIC GROWTH

1. James Dyson, "James Dyson's Advice to the Class of 2022 at Opening of the Dyson STEAM Building, Gresham's School," YouTube video, July 3, 2022, 1:30, https://www.youtube.com/watch?v=6XcQC8Oq9Jw.

2. James Dyson, *Against the Odds: An Autobiography, 2nd ed.* (Texere, 2003).

3. Stephanie Sarazin, *Soulbroken: A Guidebook for Your Journey through Ambiguous Grief* (Balance, 2022).

9. THE SCIENCE OF SERENDIPITY

1. Kevin Graham, *Ralph Nader: Battling for Democracy* (Windom Pub, 2000).

2. Mark Green, "How Ralph Nader Changed America," *The Nation*, December 1, 2015, https://www.thenation.com/article/archive/how-ralph-nader-changed-america/.

3. *Jurassic Park,* directed by Steven Spielberg, music by John Williams, Artie Kane, John Neufeld, and Alexander Courage, USA, 1993.

ACKNOWLEDGMENTS

The challenge in writing an acknowledgments section for a book of this nature is that *everyone* I've ever met–and many whom I have not–have likely played a part in shaping my life as it is today. We never know where the next catalyst will come from, and I am thankful for each one that does.

Luck has a tendency to work much better when you're allowed to let it work in your favor; I am especially grateful to those of you who took a chance on me, either personally or professionally, throughout the course of my life.

Amanda – this work would never have happened without your talents and counsel.

And you, dear reader. However you found this book I'm thankful that you've trusted me with your time. I hope I've made it worth it for you.

ABOUT THE AUTHOR

Adam Tank is a microbiologist-turned-entrepreneur, public speaker, and executive consultant whose career has spanned leadership roles in Fortune 100 companies, international small businesses, and venture capital backed technology startups. He is the founder of Tank Consulting and an executive at a VC-backed generative design SaaS startup whose software enables capital planners, project developers, and engineering professionals to rapidly generate preliminary engineering designs for critical infrastructure, including a variety of water and power assets. Through his various business ventures, his companies have impacted over 150 million people in over one hundred countries.

Adam is an engaging speaker who has entertained over 50,000 people at more than fifty events. He is a sought-after presenter and coach on topics including how to find product-market fit for early stage companies, how to give presentations that don't suck, how to determine whether graduate school is worth the investment, and how to speak a foreign language fluently in three months or less. In addition to his in-person engagements, he has millions of views across various social media platforms, and his podcast and newsletters reach over 40,000 people. He has lived in seven states and three countries and enjoys the thrill of being outside his comfort zone.

Beyond his professional work, Adam believes in serving his community as a husband, father, foster parent, volunteer for Big Brothers and Big Sisters of America, and mentor to currently and formerly incarcerated people.

For speaking, consulting, and other inquiries, visit https://adamtank.com